"*Loud & Cl[...]*
neurs to the C-Suite

—Robert Dilenschneider, CEO, The Dilenschneider Group

"*Loud & Clear* is a must read for anyone in need of *real* results—from a few essential hints to a communicative make-over. Berg's keen insights and tactical advice will definitely "*turbo-charge*" your ability to deliver an on-target message!"

—Patrick J. Collins, PhD, professor of speech and media studies at New York's John Jay College and author of *Negotiate to Win!*

"Whether you're training a junior account executive in presentation skills or media training a CEO in the middle of a PR crisis, Karen Berg delivers, helping find a winning bottom-line message no matter the need."

—John Frazier, executive vice president, Quinn & Co.

"Clarity, experience, and insight for coping with modern workplace communication issues."

—Art Stevens, managing partner, Stevens, Gould, Pincus

"The next best thing to having Karen coach you personally is to read her book, *Loud & Clear*. Her communication techniques have helped my students enormously and her illustrations are both instructional and fun."

—Jack Domeischel, adjunct professor, New York University Business School of Continuing and Professional Studies

"In today's Global Society of cultural diversity, electronic clutter and shorter attention spans, persuasive communication skills are of critical importance and a daunting challenge for any executive. Loud & Clear provides a practical framework to capture any audience attention, whether one or many, and get them to connect, engage and take the desired action. Karen Berg makes this an easy read with simple and practical examples."

—Paul G. Pochtar RPh, vice president of Oncology Managed Markets, Novartis Pharmaceuticals Corporation

KAREN BERG

L&UD
CLEAR

5 Steps to Say What You Mean and Get What You Want

CAREER PRESS   The Career Press, Inc.
Franklin Lakes, N.J.

LOUD & CLEAR
EDITED AND TYPESET BY GINA TALUCCI
Cover design by Rob Johnson/Johnson Design
Printed in the U.S.A. by Book-mart Press

To order this title, please call toll-free 1-800-CAREER-1 (NJ and Canada: 201-848-0310) to order using VISA or MasterCard, or for further information on books from Career Press.

The Career Press, Inc., 3 Tice Road, PO Box 687,
Franklin Lakes, NJ 07417
www.careerpress.com

Library of Congress Cataloging-in-Publication Data

Berg, Karen (Karen E.)
    Loud & clear : 5 steps to say what you mean and get what you want
    / by Karen Berg.
        p. cm.
    Includes index.
    ISBN 978-1-56414-987-9
        1. Business communication. 2. Oral communication. 3. Public
    speaking. 4. Interpersonal communication. I. Title. II. Title: Loud
    and clear.

    HF5718.B467 2008
    658.4′ 52--dc22

                                                    2007050409

DEDICATION AND ACKNOWLEDGMENTS

*To my clients and colleagues, who help make
my life a fabulous adventure.*

I would like to thank the following people for all their efforts and support. Without them, this book would not have been possible.

Thank you to Francine LaSala, whose talent and diligence helped birth this book. Thank you also to my agent, Sharon Bowers, for believing in me and working so hard on my behalf.

Career Press took this book on and put it into print. A special thanks to Adam Schwartz, Michael Pye, Laurie Kelly-Pye, Jeff Piasky, Kristen Parkes, Kirsten Dalley, Diana Ghazzawi, and Gina Talucci.

Phil Hall's humor, talent, and teaching ability inspires me everyday. And speaking of inspiration, a huge thank you goes out to all the professionals who gave their precious time and lent invaluable insight for Rabbit Tricks, Tips From the Trenches, Views from the Road, and more: Rock Albers, Jack Cloonan, Jerry Cole, Merrill B. Corry, Lester Davis, Patricia Diaz Dennis, Rob Faley, John Frazier, John Graves, Phil Hall, Steve Kyler, Dennis Lonergan, Dr. Cherie Marshall, Byron Nease, Dr. Don Nelson, Cabot Parsons, Michael Platt, Donna Ramer, Mary Jo Roberts, David Schwartz, Art Stevens, and Patreicia West.

And a very special thank you to Richard Berg, Dawn Butcher, Jerry Cole (for being there for me), and my family and friends, who have supported my efforts and have believed in me.

CONTENTS

INTRODUCTION

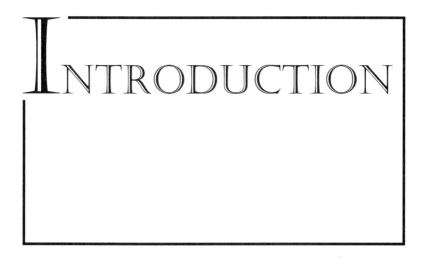

**"The average American attention span is that of a
ferret on a double espresso."
——Dennis Miller, comedian**

A while back, I was conducting a training session for a
group of female executives, handpicked by the CEO to launch
their company's new division. The meeting was called a "Lunch
Launch," though, as I would find out only too late, that meant
bring your own.

In any case, the women paraded in with their sandwiches,
salads, Diet Cokes, and bags of chips, chatting cordially as
they set up their food. They seemed civilized enough. But as
soon as the group "leader" stood up and opened her mouth, I
quickly learned this meeting was to be anything but.

Her blue eyes bulging—almost cartoon-like—she looked
at me and launched her agenda. "I don't know what you're
planning to do here today, but I have an agenda," she began.
"And we have to get all this done," she continued. "And I'd

like to know what we're supposed to be doing here with so many other things that need to get done!" At this point she was practically screaming, and half the group shut down. The other half was gearing up to state their own agendas. Once she stopped speaking, it was similar to when the bell at the New York Stock Exchange sounds; the women went wild:

"Marketing should have been in on this from the beginning! Why weren't we notified!?"

"Operations will never be able to make those dates!"

"Creative is drowning already and we're not going to kiss your butt anymore!"

"I said no mayo on this sandwich! Why is there *mayo* on this sandwich?!"

It was like a movie. As frustration mounted, each began screaming louder to be heard, yet no one was making even the smallest dent in the din.

As facilitator and trainer, of course, I had to do something, but what? My presentation to them hadn't even begun, and already the train was running off the rails. I listened to it for about five minutes and then I had to act. I stood up, held up my hands, palms facing outward, took a deep breath, and yelled: "STOP!"

Well that was one way to be *loud and clear*. In this case, it worked, because I was able to take back the meeting. Everyone was so fixated on their own issues; they needed a jolt to shake them back to reality. But in the long term, shouting is not the best way to get the attention of your listeners.

Haven't you been in this situation hundreds of times—a complete cacophony of chaos, a mess of miscommunication, that always ends up in an hour or two of wasted time, with little getting resolved?

We can all relate—especially in this day and age. We all know the feeling of no one listening when we speak, whether they're speaking right over our words, or, worse, simply nodding in our general direction, staring blankly, looking like they'd rather be anywhere else than taking in what we have to say.

We live in a manic, mile-a-minute, multitasking world, where people are bogged down in a thousand other things, scattered, fragmented, and often unable to focus.

Think about it. In the time it took you to read to this point, how many e-mails have you received? How many times has your phone rung? How many meetings have you already attended today—and how many more await you? How much attention are *you* even paying to any of it?

The world is full of noise, a constant buzzing of duties and deadlines, worries and wants, stresses and obligations, which make it nearly impossible for anyone to absorb any more information: e-mail and the Internet, BlackBerrys and iPhones, globalization, and telecommuting. Blurred lines between when it's work time and when it's time off. If it's not creating a work-family balance, it's the fear of being phased out or made obsolete thanks to outsourcing. There's only so much the human mind can process.

But through all this "noise," you still have to find a way to make your own voice heard if you're ever going to get anywhere.

Don't worry. I can show you how.

Speak Up!

Everyone has strengths and weaknesses when it comes to communicating. No person is good at it all the time, and most people fear it altogether. In fact, public speaking is the number-one fear of Americans—rated higher than dying, divorce, and bankruptcy. But whether you're addressing one, 10, 100, or 1,000 people, you still have to do it, so you'd better find a way to do it right. How? As esteemed PR pro Art Stevens, managing partner of StevensGouldPincus, once told me, you have to "grab them by the shoulders" and never let go.

You want your boss to focus on your pet project. You need your college professor to write a glowing recommendation for your summer internship. You'd like your neighbor to prune back an unruly tree blocking your view. You want an airplane employee to get you on a flight. *Loud & Clear* will help you get your voice heard.

Why You?

Because it's high time you became a better communicator. Remember: how you communicate is a direct link to professional—and personal—success. And who deserves these more than you?

Why Me?

...because I've been at this for more than 20 years, helping all kinds of people, from the executive to the entry level. Whether it's NASA astronauts, engineers at think tanks, celebrities, authors, politicians, and even regular folks trying to save their local park or sway their PTA, I've helped thousands tailor and deliver effective, results-driven messages. For the past several years, I've interviewed numerous professionals and met with hundreds of people a week, and asked them what they felt was working in today's communication environment and what wasn't. That, combined with my own experience, is how I can help you.

Why Now?

Because there has never been a worse time to try and express anything to anyone with all the other distractions constantly buzzing around. Eventually, the trend may shift toward "unplugging." In fact, a 2006 survey by the Association of Executive Search Consultants found "half of senior executives polled would go so far as to turn down a promotion if it meant losing control of their schedule" (as reported by Lisa Belkin in the *New York Times*). But we're still a long way from that, so until we get there, stick with me.

The Loud & Clear Approach

Communicating effectively comes down to five simple strategies, which anyone can easily master:

1. **Probe.** Before you open your mouth to speak, you'd better know exactly who you're addressing, and exactly what they'll need to hear from you. Not only will this enable you to connect with them, you'll make them actually *want* to listen, and even act on your behalf.

2. **Position.** How you organize your information affects how others receive it, so, once you know to whom you're talking, it's time to use your head and brainstorm what you need to say and how to say it.

3. **Persuade.** If they don't like you, don't trust you, or can't understand you, they ain't gonna buy what you're selling. By mastering the four cornerstones of communication—clarity, consistency, chemistry, and credibility—you'll keep their interest, and keep it interesting.

4. **Perform.** How can you compete with cell phones and numerous other distractions, and also ensure your message will stick the way you want it to? I'll show you why visual images—mental or actual physical pieces, are important devices—and how to use them effectively. I'll also share appearance secrets, plus speech and body language techniques that make a lasting impression.

5. **Preempt.** Where there's smoke, there's fire, and where there's a message to be delivered, you can bet some obstacle is going to get in the way. I'll show you how to anticipate disaster before it strikes, and how to cope and get back in control when the meeting sours, or something unusual occurs.

I'm not out to make more noise for you; I've organized this material in a format that will be easy to read and digest. In addition to general information and colorful case studies, you will find:

Noise Blasters. Quick, solution-oriented tip boxes.

5-Minute Plans of Attack. Quick sanity savers mapped out by the minute.

Rabbit Tricks. These "damage control" boxes show how to salvage a communications situation gone awry.

Tough-Love Turnarounds. My take-no-prisoners approach to common communication cop-outs, and how to stop crippling yourself with them.

Tips From the Trenches. Interviews with top communicators on everything from how to use your voice to how to be a better listener to how to dress the part, and much more.

Yes, we'll do worksheets. Sure, we'll plot charts. And we'll work together to change the way you communicate for good.

If you need something from one person, if you need the attention of 100 people, if you want people to care about what you have to say and actually act on your agenda, yours has to be the voice that stands out. There has to be clear, static-free communication of your thoughts and needs to get what you want—your career and your quality of life absolutely depend on it.

By the time we get to the end of this book, you'll know exactly how to communicate over all that noise and finally express yourself, *Loud & Clear* and—fingers crossed—without ever having to raise your voice.

I want to hear from you. Please visit me at *www. CommCoreStrategies.com* to share your communication horror stories and catch advice from the front lines. I'd also like to hear how this book helped you, or even how it didn't. E-mail me at KBerg@CommCoreStrategies.com.

Good luck!
Karen Berg

STRATEGY 1

PROBE:
Targeting Your Audience

"The only normal people are the ones
you don't know too well."
—Rodney Dangerfield

While Rodney Dangerfield was looking for laughs with this quip, there's actually a lot of wisdom in it. It hits on something of which we're all guilty most of the time: assuming who others are. We assume that they're just like us, and we deal with them on that level, never getting to know who they really are. When you deal with others without first getting to know their agenda and what they *need* to hear in order to motivate them, you're only going to get one place with them: nowhere.

This brings us to my first strategy: Probe. Remember that when I use the term *audience* in this book, I'm talking about anyone to whom you need to deliver a message. It's not public speaking, it's communication—whether you're asking your boss for a raise, hosting a small meeting to push one of your projects through, or even making your case in front of the PTA. It doesn't really matter how many people you're talking to. If you don't take the time to get to know them and what makes them tick before you open your mouth, chances are they won't listen to you.

And, when you think about it, why should they? If someone rambled on and on at you, never taking into consideration your level of interest in the topic, or how it affects you, would you care? Be honest. You know you'd tune out, and likely usually do. Forget even going out of your way for that person— would you make even the smallest effort to help him or her advance an agenda if his or her cause didn't benefit you in some way? It's the number-one rule of effective communication: When you ignore people who have agendas separate from yours, you're guaranteed to be speaking on deaf ears.

So why don't we take the time to get to know people and understand where they're coming from before we speak to them? Maybe we're afraid to get too close, to cross boundaries— real or perceived—for fear we'll come across as naïve, pushy, or even, as Dangerfield suggests, abnormal. Maybe we feel like we don't have the time to do this kind of research as we race from one meeting to another.

Guess what? You have to make time. The good thing is it doesn't take as much time as you think, and the payoff is well worth the investment. Now more than ever, especially in this overbooked, overwrought world, you need to take a step back and probe the interests of your listeners. Find out what you can offer them in exchange for five, 10, 30, or 60 minutes of their time. By taking the time to get to know the people, you'll see most everyone has their quirks, idiosyncrasies, and preferences, and, if you consider these as you craft your message, you're going to get results.

In this chapter, I'll show you how easy it is to get inside the heads of others and really speak to them—to make people feel that even in a large group, you're only addressing them individually and have their best interests at heart. By the time you reach the end of this chapter, you will:

- ¤ learn how to profile an "audience" of any size, from one to 1,000.
- ¤ plot a graph that will show, at a glace, the agendas of others.
- ¤ get an introduction in how to speak across cultural boundaries.
- ¤ discover how to deliver bad, even potentially life-shattering news with smarts, sensitivity, and savvy.

NOISE BLASTER!

Little touches make big impressions. The more often you reference concrete aspects of your listeners' lives—names, places, events, situations—the more you'll make them feel as though you are one of them.

TIPS FROM THE TRENCHES

Patreicia West

"When I need to address anyone, I first write down what my objective should be in the context in which I am working. It is important to distinguish between what the objective should be, what the situation is calling for, and what I want to see as my objective. I may want to see the group or individual I'm working with do certain things because that is the way I would do it, however, that may not be what is most appropriate given the circumstances. If my role is to help people do their best thinking and come to the best decisions for *them*, then an objective to convince them to do what I think is best is the wrong objective.

Step two is to think about where that person or group is in relationship to the issue, concern, work, opportunity, and so forth. I then get a better idea of (1) what I need to understand and formulate questions around, and (2) what are the critical points I must share/offer to move the process forward. I also need to assess how what I have to offer can support what I think would be their objective."

Who *Are* These People?

It doesn't matter if you want a raise from your employer or if you need to reprimand a subordinate. To get the results you want, you have to do the legwork. You have to figure out to whom you're talking, and develop a message that speaks specifically to them.

Say you need to have a word with an employee; for our purposes, let's call him Steve. He's been underperforming lately. Maybe he's been coming in late frequently or missing deadlines, or not cooperating with his colleagues.

No one enjoys being reprimanded, and most people will react defensively when this thankless task falls to you. Now you have to figure out how you're going to deal with Steve. He may get angry and lash out at you, blaming the problem on your "poor managerial skills." He may blame another coworker who's making him look bad. He may get upset, bawling away as you try to make your point through the waterworks, all the while trying not to hate yourself too much for inflicting such pain and suffering on another human being. He may clam up, having no response for you whatsoever, but, in his mind, he'll be planning his revenge and your downfall. It goes without saying that each of these scenarios requires a different touch.

Before you have to face Steve, find out about him. Who is he? How has he dealt with discipline before? Does he have a criminal record? You get the point.

Following is a "listener's profile," which offers questions you can ask yourself as you get to know others, and what they're going to need from you:

- ⌑ **Knowledge.** Does Steve know his job duties and what your expectations of him are? Is he aware that you, as well as his colleagues, have noticed a decline in his performance? Have there been any prior warnings?

- ⌑ **Needs.** Has Steve made any requests to you— additional staff or time to complete a project? More funding in the budget for his department?

- ⌑ **Age.** Is he older than you? If so, he may feel out-raged (on some level) that you're in charge of him, even though he's been at it a lot longer than you. Is he younger than you? If so, he may feel threatened that you have more experience than him, and you know ways to make his workaday life a living hell. Or worse, maybe he's fresh out of school, perhaps has a higher degree, and thinks he knows everything? (See Tough-Love TurnAround: The Know-It-All on page 26.)

¤ **Gender.** If you are a female, is he the type who believes somehow his being a man already sets him on a level above you? Or does he feel he can flirt with you and somehow charm away your dissatisfaction? If you are also male, is he the type that constantly vies for the alpha position?

¤ **Nationality.** In this globalized workplace, it isn't uncommon for us to be working side by side with people from other countries and cultures, who may have different ideas about what should be expected of them in the workplace. (Just try telling someone who lived in the Mediterranean region, who's used to slowing down in the afternoon and has a different work rhythm, that it's *expected* for him or her to work through lunch.) We'll get into this a bit more later. (See Excursions in Unfamiliar Territory on page 41.)

¤ **Temperament.** Is Steve someone who easily flies off the handle? Is he generally easygoing and even-tempered? Again, how has he reacted to criticism in the past? How has he handled a disagreement with another coworker?

¤ **Family.** Is he married—and are you? Does he have children—and do you? On a professional level, none of this is any of your business. But if you can find common ground on a personal level (perhaps your kids are the same ages or your spouses do the cooking at home, even if you have cats or dogs or any other pets), you can use these things to break the ice and try and forge a "comfort zone."

⌗ **Outside interests.** What does he do when he isn't at work? Again, on a professional level, none of your business. But if you can connect through a shared love of books, the theater, sports, or even kite-flying, it will only help you in making him see that you're "on his team," and that you're not attacking him simply because you don't like him (whether you do or not).

You may be saying to yourself, "Hey, some of this seems pretty manipulative." And on some level, you're right. Finding out how to work with people to get what you want could be viewed as manipulation, but it's also smart communication. And what it all comes down to is that the better you are at finding common ground with a person and connecting with them, the more effective you're going to be when it comes to delivering a message—good news or bad.

What are some common things you can bond over?

⌗ **Family.** You don't have to air the family laundry, but if you have kids the same age and can share similar experiences, you have great common ground.

⌗ **Hobbies.** Do you like knitting? Stamp collecting? The things you do in your spare time could help open new doors of communication you never knew existed.

⌗ **Pets.** Do you have a dog or a cat or even something more exotic like a bird or reptile? People love to talk about their pets, sometimes more than their families, and this is a great way to bond with another person.

¤   **Sports.** Taking five minutes to talk about last night's game isn't going to lose the company any revenue. And bonding with people who like the same teams as you makes them want to be around you. Conversely, a playful rivalry sparked by a passion for opposing teams will also have people seeking you out—if only to gloat over their team being in a better position than yours. It's still a door for open communication.

¤   **Film, T.V., books.** Again, it's all about finding common interest. A weekly T.V. show you can talk about before the day begins or before a meeting keeps you bonded with your coworkers and keeps communication free and easy.

Tap into what interests people; focus your messages to appeal to these interests, and you'll win every time.

Overall, never guess the information. Don't expect that a woman likes shopping, a man follows football, or even that all parents enjoy talking about parenting. If you don't know something about a person, find someone who does and ask them. In the case of Steve, if you don't know what his "hot button" points are, find from someone who does. In what other departments has he worked? For which other supervisors has he worked?

Before you call Steve into your office, be sure you've thought through just how to approach the subject and how you will deal with any opposition from him. What happens if he gets defensive and threatens to quit—or to go over your head? With whom can you build an alliance to help smooth out any rough patches that may arise? Prepare yourself beforehand, probing to find out everything you can, and you'll be much better equipped to diffuse any bombs you may set off. We'll get deeper into being prepared for anything when we get to the last strategy, which is *preempt*.

TOUGH-LOVE TURNAROUND:
THE KNOW-IT-ALL

You say: I recently joined the firm and I have a doctorate from Harvard. I think these people should take my suggestions, but they just won't listen to me.

I say: I have three words for you, and they all have to do with probing: attitude, acknowledge, and approach.

First of all, congratulations on graduating from Harvard; it is an impressive school, but it's time to check your attitude at the door. You're now in the business world, not in the classroom, and things are happening in real time, not neatly mapped out in the pages of a textbook. The people you're trying to impress have been in this "real world" much longer than you have. For years, they've been slogging through, trying to make the best decisions possible to help the business run as well as keep their jobs.

Step back from your degree for a minute and *acknowledge* that you don't know everything, but you do know something. Think about how you can translate what you do know into workable ways to improve the professional lives and situations of these specific people—they're not models you read about in your sociology class case studies.

Now, work on your *approach*. Try saddling up in a non-intimidating way—the "we're all in this together" approach goes a long way to win supporters. People generally want new ideas and fresh thinking; they just don't want it forced on them by some newbie who hasn't bothered to take the time to learn the ropes at their particular organization. That will shut down the crowd every time.

Crowded House

I've said it before and I'll probably say it 100 more times if I have to: Even if you're addressing people you already know, you still need to probe your listener. Not doing so can backfire on you, which happened to Andrea, a client of mine (see page 30).

Getting to know about one person isn't very difficult at all. When you're dealing with a small group of people, you have more challenges than looking into just one person, just in terms of volume, but you also have the added bonus that people generally know the same people. If you ask Dan's good friend Cheryl about Dan, and Dan is really good friends with Eric, chances are Cheryl knows Eric as well...two birds, one stone.

When you have a large group to deal with, it just doesn't make sense to go out and find out about everyone who will be in the audience. In situations such as these, you have to rely on generalizations—not broad, sweeping, stereotype-driven ones, but ones you can develop, almost scientifically, by asking yourself several questions about the group and hitting on their prime demographics.

The following worksheet can serve as a guideline for you to suss out the needs of any size group—even a small one—and probe for a general agenda. If you have enough information about the group to make the questions more specific for yourself, great!

Worksheet: Discover Your Audience

1. What is my relationship with the person or group I need to address?

   _____

2. How much do they already know about me?

   _____

3. Are they my peers, superiors, subordinates, or a mix?

   _____

4. How much credibility do I have with the audience, and vice versa? (That is, my age, gender, culture, race, experience, and knowledge of the subject compared to theirs.)

   _____

5. What is my purpose—to inform, to sell, to per-
    suade, to motivate, anger, frighten, harmonize,
    neutralize, or to create controversy?

    _____

6. What do they want from me in terms of financial,
    informational, or emotional support?

    _____

7. What do I want from them?

    _____

8. What other factors may be influencing how I see
    the audience? (That is, my own personal, finan-
    cial, or emotional needs.)

    _____

9. What other factors may be influencing how they
    see me?

    _____

10. Why should they care about what I have to say?

    _____

Anticipating the Agendas of Others

What happens when you don't take the time to scope out
your audience and figure out how to keep them on board

before you open your mouth? My client, Andrea, had to find out the hard way.

A senior manager of a large, global pharmaceutical company, she was told by her boss to put together a group for a special task: The company needed to boost the sales of one of their older medications to pump up revenue until some of the newer drugs in the research pipeline were ready for release.

Without a moment's hesitation, Andrea selected a dozen employees, who were not her direct reports, and called them in for an urgent meeting.

After the group assembled, she explained she had just been given a project that called for extra work on everyone's part. Then she launched right into the cold, hard facts: There would be long hours involved for the next several weeks, without extra pay.

Andrea assumed she'd have her team's support. While she hadn't worked directly with these people, she worked in the same company with them for years. Surely they knew how important it was for all of them to dazzle the higher-ups by acing this task.

But the group's reaction was not quite what she expected; not only were they unsupportive, but they became rebellious as well. One of the members, Joe, glared at her and said bluntly, "You're the global manager. You figure it out." He then strode out of the room.

The group, thoroughly demoralized, then broke up the meeting without any resolution.

What went wrong? Andrea had delivered her directive to a group of people who were already busier and more stressed than they could comfortably handle. Because she didn't probe and anticipate their concerns beforehand, taking just a few minutes to analyze what they might accept as fair and reasonable, she failed to shape her message correctly.

Joe had grasped the negatives immediately: No one was going to get a raise for doing this extra job; no one was going to be intellectually challenged by coming up with some new sales strategy; no one was being offered lighter responsibilities elsewhere in exchange; and no one was going to be showered with glory for pumping a little more life into a drug whose future was of short duration at best. Not only could he find no self-serving reason to make him want to extend himself or be cooperative, he swayed the others to his side.

NOISE BLASTER!

Even if you're friendly with colleagues with whom you've worked on other teams or with whom you socialize—especially if they're members of your own family—you need to start from ground zero when you become the leader of a group. Before you start making demands, step back and analyze who they are and what motivates them in order to sway them to your side.

What's in It for *Me*?

Right off the bat, you absolutely must present your listeners with brief but compelling information that outlines what is in it for them, why they should care, and why you are the person who can deliver the goods. If you're not a rock star or celebrity, your audience isn't there to hear you perform and pontificate. They want to know what they stand to gain from what you have to offer. They need to be sold on you, and your job is to make sure they do feel they're getting something for themselves—even if they aren't.

"It's worth asking: what do you want? It gets harder to answer as you get older. The answer gets subtler and subtler."
——John Jerome, writer

NOISE BLASTER!

Personalization adds dimension. If you're meeting people in a different city, go the extra mile and learn something unique about that city— a nugget of obscure history, a little-known but much-revered restaurant. The personal touch makes it seem like it's about "us"—not just about the speaker.

Changing Obstacles Into Opportunities

When Andrea sought out my advice, I told her exactly what happened: she came on too strong, and neglected to evaluate beforehand if there were any benefits she could come up with to soften the blow. Then, I showed her how to salvage her project.

I introduced a simple, quick analytical grid for her to pin-point each team member's special needs, which follows on page 34. I call it a W.I.I.F.M (what's in it for me?) grid, and in all my years doing this, it has proven to be one of the most essential tools in my arsenal. Once filled out, it shows you everything you need to know about a group—and at a quick glance. And you don't need any expertise in any kind of sophisticated chart-making software to use it. Draw it on a piece of scrap paper or the back of a file or envelope if you have to.

Once I showed Andrea this grid, she shook her head and said: "It's so simple." And it is. The beauty of seeing all the obstacles on one page is that you will find commonalities among

the staffers and this will help you lead to better solutions and task allocation.

What's in It for Me (W.I.I.F.M.) Grid

Name	Obstacles	Incentives
Joe		
Lisa		
Frank		
Paul		
Maria		
Christine		
Stephanie		
Shawn		
Ralph		
Jack		

Within minutes, Andrea had the whole situation spelled out and, at a glance, knew what she was up against. She could also see concrete solutions she could offer team members to make them less resentful about doing the extra work. When she analyzed that the medical director was already up to his eyeballs in medical reports, she knew she had to make the most of his limited time. She figured out that if she could just get his attention for one hour a week, she could get what she needed from him—without making him feel like he was "giving away" too much of his time. The same applied with the others. She saw that if she could minimize the time commitment they needed to make, and maximize the limited amount of time they could give, she could earn their dedication to the project.

5-MINUTE PLAN OF ATTACK

As Andrea learned, it takes literally minutes to analyze a group and come up with ways to satisfy the needs of others. Say you just got handed a huge and important project that's already behind deadline, and you have to assemble a team to get it done. Now, once you know who's going to be recruited to help you save the day, it's time to act.

Minute 1: Step outside yourself and start to imagine what it feels like to be one of your listeners.

Minute 2: Consider their distractions—the e-mail, papers, and phone messages piling up, as they skip lunch to try and leave at a reasonable enough hour to have dinner with their families.

Minute 3: Alongside all the other stuff with which they have to contend, ask yourself what's in it for them (W.I.I.F.M.)—and why should they be bothered listening to you.

> **Minutes 4-5**: Sketch out the W.I.I.F.M. grid (see page 34) and map out their obstacles, as well as the solutions or incentives you can offer them.
>
> You now have a tool to help you maximize the enthusiasm and efforts of your team, and at the same time, that will help minimize any resentment or frustration on team members' parts about having to drop everything for you.

With her audience's needs and motivations now clear in her mind, Andrea was able to go back to each of the people on her team, and show them how they could gain some advantage of their own while making a meaningful contribution. This time, she won the willing support of virtually everyone on the team.

Stranger in a Strange Land

As it was for Andrea, sometimes you'll know the people or person with whom you need to speak—even if just in passing. In these situations, you can safely and confidently rely on the W.I.I.F.M. grid to outline and analyze your listeners' agendas, essentially filling in the blanks off the top of your head, and tailor your message to appeal to these agendas.

But sometimes you'll have to talk to people you don't know at all. If you don't already know the players and their agendas, you still have to do the legwork to get to know them.

Imagine you're a campaigning politician. Before making any speeches or shaking any hands, the smart office-seeker sends an advance team to look over the territory, take the local pulse, and discover the issues and concerns of their potential constituencies. That way, when the politician arrives, he or she can at least attempt to address their interests in relevant ways. You don't have to pay someone to do your prospecting. There are plenty of other resources available to you:

- ¤ **E-mail or phone ahead.** Get information including the size of the group, the time of day, the location of the presentation, and your place in the day's program. All of these factors can affect your audience's receptivity.

- ¤ **Contact audience members.** If possible, draw out information about the group to help you prepare your audience profile. If the group is very small, try to have at least a brief conversation with each person before the meeting to anticipate objections or questions that may be raised, and how you can answer them before they rise to object.

- ¤ **Research the group.** Learn what they already know about your subject, what biases and attitudes they bring to the party, and what their levels of expertise are. This will tell you whether technical language and concepts can be used in your presentation, or whether your material needs to be delivered in simplified language and business-related anecdotes. And it will also tell you whether you will need to educate your listeners as well as persuade or suggest.

✤ **Know their interests.** Find out how their immedi-
ate and long-term concerns will relate to your
topic. For example, if you're proposing a major
change, research the history of the organization
and how the change may fit into their current
activities.

✤ **Get there early.** Arrive hours in advance, if possible. If you have to speak in another city, get
there the day before. Take time to check things
out. Make sure everything's compatible with your
software, and that the equipment you'll be rely-
ing on—the microphone, overhead projector, and
so forth—actually works.

✤ **Track down the influencers.** Find out who is most
important to win over, either because of their position in the company or their personality. Are
they argumentative just to make a point? Are they
competitive or jealous? Seek out these people and
try and give each a brief preview of your presentation, and get their input before you speak. This
will show respect and also give them an investment in the outcome of your presentation.

✤ **Dress the part.** Find out if the office is formal or
casual and dress accordingly. Just keep in mind
that business casual is different for every company. Some may see it as meaning jeans and sneakers; others consider casual to mean jacket, no tie.

RABBIT TRICK:
LAST-MINUTE STRATEGY ADJUSTMENT

Problem: After several weeks of thought and preparation, you're ready to pitch a story idea to the editor of a magazine you've been reading forever. You've even been able to land an in-person interview with this editor. The morning of the interview, you get a phone call from the editor's assistant. She says that the person you've spent all your time getting to know was fired last week, but her replacement still wants to see you. Trouble is, you have no idea who this person is. What do you do?

Solution: Just as you did when learning about the editor and figuring out how you might address her, so you must do now—albeit at an accelerated pace. Speak to the assistant and find out what she knows about her new boss. You may be able to find out if that person prefers formal or informal presentations. Does he or she like to ask a lot of questions? Get the person's name—and make sure you get the correct spelling—and Google him or her immediately to find out whatever you can. Maybe you'll come across trade newsletters or even a MySpace page. Read whatever you can, quickly and carefully. Store away interesting pieces of information for making conversation when you meet the person. ("I understand you worked for Sarah Jones. What was that like?") You'll give that person an opportunity to say something about herself, and you may be able to find common ground on which you can connect.

Worksheet: The Setting

Where you relay your message can impact your listeners almost as much as what you want to say and how you say it. Here are some questions to ask yourself about the venue in which you'll be speaking as you develop your message.

1. Where will I be presenting my ideas or arguments—their turf, my turf, or neutral turf?

2. What time of day, and what day of week, am I scheduled to meet with my listeners?

3. Will they—or I—be compromised by jetlag?

4. Is there a dress code?

5. How comfortable will I be in formal or in dress-down attire?

6. If this is an international group, what countries are being represented? Do you understand these cultures? Do you need to do additional research, such as reading books about the culture or cultures, before addressing the group?

7. How well does my audience understand my language, and how will this affect my presentation? (That is, should it be more visually oriented, have simple vocabulary, and so on.)

8. Will the discussion take place in person or remotely, online or on the telephone, through an audio or video conference call?

9. If it's a video conference, is it one- or two-way video?

10. If there is no visual component, will my message still work without graphics?

11. If there is no visual component, what can I substitute?

Now you can visualize actually delivering your presentation to your audience, which will help you develop a more thoughtful, provocative message.

Excursions in Unfamiliar Territory

In this ever-expanding global environment, it's more likely than not that you will be involved in meetings with people overseas, perhaps even traveling long distances and crossing many time zones to talk to diverse audiences scattered over several continents. Whether you're there in person, or via phone, teleconference, or even e-mail, you need to prepare, take control, and build a relationship quickly.

Always plan for the worst. Maybe you've assumed you'll be selling your message to a select audience of two dozen managers around a table, but instead find the entire staff has gathered to hear you. Sometimes there's a technological snafu: Your demonstration material, supposedly shipped as baggage aboard your plane, has inexplicably ended up a thousand miles away, with no chance of being rerouted in time for your presentation. We'll get more involved in anticipating disaster and planning appropriately in Chapter 5.

NOISE BLASTER!

Make it a rule, at least for your first meeting with a client or company, to dress one notch above their standard dress code.

Crossing Cultural Borders

Gestures, phrases, values, etiquette, and appropriate body language vary from one culture to the next, so you risk losing audiences if you deliver the same message in the same manner wherever you go. In government circles, it's called protocol, and diplomats get intensive training in the do's and don'ts of the countries to which they are posted. Nowadays, we are all diplomats to some degree, and you must never forget that one country's good manners may be another's faux pas.

TIPS FROM THE TRENCHES

Lester Davis
president, Basilio Advantage

"People on this side of the pond [Europe] have a different business culture. Most meetings are in-person, and while everyone uses e-mail, they unplug at lunchtime, at the end of the day, on weekends, and on holidays (which they typically take for two weeks at a time without any business contact). For you, this could be very good news. Just because your fellow North Americans don't unplug from time to time does not mean you need to follow suit. Similar to the Europeans, you can define the parameters for contact. (Twice-a-day summary e-mails, giving clear blackout times in which you are not available, create the structure so you are not scrambling to catch up with an endless avalanche of communications.) And if you want to stay plugged in all the time, that's your prerogative, too. Just be aware that people with whom you do business across the pond, and even within your own division, may not be available as you want them to be.

> In order to win them, to connect to them and make them want to interact with you, you need to respect their parameters." Before you start making demands, step back and analyze who they are. Find out what motivates them in order to sway them to your side.

Entering a Different Generational Zone

Oceans and boundaries and languages aside, some of the biggest culture clashes happen within cultures—and across generations. This is particularly true in the areas of the dotcoms and e-commerce, where Gen-Xers and Gen-Yers often find themselves butting heads with Boomer leaders and managers who provide some of the capital, marketing, and distribution know-how. Problems arise not just in the area of technology, but in learning and work style, language, and manners as well.

For that reason, you need to know how to talk to people in every generation. There are things a 25-year-old should never say to a 50-year-old, and vice versa. We'll get into some of those hot-button phrases a bit later as we examine how understanding the working and thinking habits of one another is essential in forging communications connections.

Problems arise in communication between the generations because many people aren't sensitive to other generations' place in life when addressing them. People just assume that their perspective is the only one, and don't understand that their words or their behavior may actually be shocking and offensive to other generations.

For instance, an older person may presume a certain degree of knowledge on a younger colleague's part, and, therefore not lay the groundwork the younger person needs. On the other hand, a younger staffer may be afraid to ask an older worker, because he feels like he should already know something, and he doesn't want to expose his inexperience. Sometimes a younger person will feel intimidated to ask an older person a question, thinking he or she should know it without "disturbing" the seasoned pro. And sometimes it's the older professional's doing—perhaps the last time the intern asked how something got done, the older one sighed and said something to the effect of, "It will be easier if I just do it." It's a two-way street.

How do people in their 20s, 30s, 40s, 50s, and older relate to other generations? Perspective is everything. Some general guidelines follow.

People in their 20s and early 30s tend to be very open about their needs and what they want from others, their careers, and their companies. Typically, they're in their first or second jobs, and are looking at their positions as resume and portfolio builders; perhaps the long-term needs of the companies they're currently with are not really a pressing concern for them. They change jobs every few years, building a general business education versus building seniority in any one business. The bottom line: If you're older, become a mentor. Teach them. Offer them new skills. If you can be a mentor, you'll have them for life.

People in their mid- to late 30s and 40s are usually at the point on their professional paths where they are in the middle in a generational sense—between older and younger colleagues—but also in a professional sense. It's likely they are in their first or second management positions, and eyeing the spots above them. They may have job-jumped a lot when they were younger, but are now trying to build a name and a career with one company, and putting in as much time as it takes.

But at this time in life, there's generally more patience than when people are in their 20s. Try helping this group as they make their way into senior management. If you're older, you can be more influential; if you're younger, you can always be supportive.

NOISE BLASTER!

A word to those in the 20s and early 30s group: Be mindful of what you post online. Coarse language, scandalous photos, and the like may come back to haunt you when a potential employer Googles you after an interview to see what you're really all about. Also, keep in mind that stuff posted on the Internet has an indefinite shelf-life. The raving anti-establishment rants that you film for YouTube now can easily be called up in 5, 10, or even 20 years. While you may be as far away from where you are now, it only takes a couple of clicks of a mouse, and it can easily be called back to incriminate you.

People in their 50s are coming from a different place, both personally and professionally. Their generation was taught to be loyal to the company and stay with it until retirement, if at all possible. They were also taught to do their jobs without complaining, and were never given the "gift" of voicing their needs. For that reason, they may become impatient with younger folks, thinking of them as whiny and entitled, which is true for most generations as you view from the golden years down to the carefree 20s. Be respectful that some people have been doing their jobs longer than you've been walking. Even if you can show this group new ways to perform old tricks, be tactful, and take those years of wisdom and experience into account when you speak.

Relationship Sabotage

If you really want to damage or end a professional relationship with someone younger or older than you, it's easy—just say the wrong thing. If you don't, take a breath and a couple of seconds before you open your mouth, and always pay attention to what you say.

What you should never say to an older colleague:

- ¤ I'm sure you don't understand technology, so I'll give this project to someone else.
- ¤ You've been coming in late—are you not feeling well?
- ¤ You're taking too much time with the customers—move it along.
- ¤ Do you have any younger people? We need fresh thinking on the team.
- ¤ Hurry it up, cut to the chase, get to the point.
- ¤ We don't do things like that anymore; that's so 1980s.

What you should never say to a younger colleague:

- ¤ When I was your age…
- ¤ Been there, done that.
- ¤ I know you've never done this before.
- ¤ This may be beyond the scope of your experience.
- ¤ How did you come up with that? Everyone knows that's unrealistic.

¤   Let me show you how to do this—it will be easier for me to show you or do it myself.

¤   What did they teach you at that college anyway?

It doesn't matter if you're in the throes of a deadline, or your kids have been up all night with the flu, or you're stretched well beyond your capacity. You have to take the time to think before you speak.

Write down the phrases you should never say, and tear that sheet of paper to shreds. Then, take the phrases you should say, and post them where you can easily refer to them—the refrigerator, your bulletin board, wherever it will be seen by you several times a day.

Whippersnapper Whips Up a Miracle

It happens all the time. A presenter of a different generation has to introduce and sell an idea to another generation—and they're not buying. Older folks may be comfortable with the old ways; younger people may think what's being proposed is inefficient or outdated.

I worked with the son of one of my clients, who was facing a situation like this. He was a 25-year-old IT guy, and, as far as the elders in his company were concerned, "fresh out of school." But as one of the younger members of the staff, he also had insights into technologies of which the older members were not familiar—technologies that would help the speed and efficiency by which they all worked.

Knowing his level of expertise in this area, his boss asked him to put together a presentation to sway the old thinking. Seeing an opportunity to really make a name for himself in the company, Alan embraced the challenge. And then he panicked.

He'd seen people his age and experience level get shot down, even humiliated, when trying to bring new ideas to the rest of the team at this company. He didn't want that to be him. Also, the innovation he was proposing was fairly high-tech, and his audience may not have known anything about it, so it could make them feel anxious and out-of-touch. Tension, hostility, and resistance would be the least of his problems.

Alan called me and explained exactly what he needed to do, and what he was up against. He needed to make a presentation to senior managers on a new state-of-the-art IT system that would improve the company's inventory control capabilities long-term. I asked him to tell me what he saw as some of the positives and negatives of the new system right off the bat.

⌗   Positives: He had every reason to believe that he was selling the right system for the right job.

⌗   Negatives: The system would be expensive to install. It would necessitate changing some well-established procedures, and cause some temporary disruptions in several departments before its benefits would be realized. And then there was the audience; people not particularly well-versed in the technology, who were probably resistant to taking advice from one half their age.

Alan anticipated there would be plenty of controversy and distrust, but he also recognized that if he could manage to overcome these hurdles and win enthusiastic support for his program, he would get an enormous boost up the corporate ladder. So we started to plan.

I advised him to list the scheduled attendees and find out who the most influential ones were, and who were most likely to be negative for whatever reason.

I then told him to analyze what particular areas of their work would be affected by the new system, and anticipate what specific benefits their management area would experience through the changeover—more efficient use of man-hours, cost-per-unit savings based on just-in-time delivery of inventory, or whatever else might be relevant. I showed him the W.I.I.F.M. grid, and he plotted out his strategy.

Before the presentation, Alan sought out key people and previewed a summary of his presentation to give each one a better understanding of the technology. Though he already knew the benefits and drawbacks, he made sure to ask for their input, and to be respectful of their comments. He called me afterward and thanked me for my advice. He now felt ready to proceed.

On the day of the meeting, Alan greeted his audience with collegiality and self-confidence. He knew that several of his listeners were solidly behind his proposal. And for others who were still unconvinced, he had previewed their major objections and prepared additional information to address those concerns. When the session ended, the majority had endorsed the new IT system, along with Alan's ability to implement it.

After the meeting, Alan's boss took him aside to express his delight that everything had gone so smoothly. "You had them eating out of your hand!" he said with amazement.

A year or more after that fateful meeting, with the new system up and running and all of the glitches ironed out, Alan got a nice raise and a very nice promotion. He was able to avoid being thrown to the wolves in a situation that helped propel him forward in his career, and all because he took the time to *probe* his audience and figure out exactly what they needed to hear. It no longer mattered that he was half their age. He had taken their perspectives into consideration, and that helped him earn not only their support, but their respect as well.

It's Not What You Say. It's How You Say It

There are many different situations in which you'll be called upon to address people who aren't your peers. But whether they are or not, you need to know exactly what to say to them—exactly what they need to hear—to get them rallying behind you. But you also need to know how to say it to appeal to various audiences and listeners. As you begin your strategy with probing, keep this fact in the back of your mind.

If you want to be an effective communicator, it's incredibly important to understand what you have to offer, and under what circumstances you need to hold back on that. But we'll get to that later.

Scoping the Territory

Jenna had just moved to a new city and joined the PTA at her daughter's school. Almost immediately, she found herself not liking the condition of the playground, which looked like it hadn't been updated in years. She wanted to see it changed.

Unfortunately, there were limited funds in the school budget, and these were being allocated to other places by Georgia, the PTA leader, who also happened to be the person responsible for selecting the original playground equipment 10 years earlier.

Jenna wanted to get her point across without stepping on Georgia's toes over her money-management decisions, or hurting her feelings by questioning the safety of the playground she had installed. She knew she had to talk to Georgia directly before she took her concerns to the committee, but she wasn't sure how.

I advised Jenna that before confronting Georgia, she'd have to lay some groundwork. I told her to first speak to other members of the committee and see how they felt about the old playground. Because these people had an existing relationship with Georgia, I urged Jenna to probe them for information about Georgia: how she liked to be approached—whether in person, by phone, or by e-mail—as well as how she had reacted to being opposed in the past.

By talking with others, Jenna learned that the best way to get through to Georgia, who, in addition to having an insanely busy schedule was also sensitive to confrontation, was to first send an e-mail. Jenna crafted a friendly note first complimenting Georgia's efforts on another committee decision, and then briefly mentioning the issues she intended to bring up about the playground at the next meeting. Unfortunately, all Georgia seemed to be able to focus on were the negatives—in other words, the fact that Jenna wanted to replace her installation was a direct attack on Georgia.

Jenna and Georgia had a back-and-forth exchange during the next couple of days, but Jenna was not making the headway she had expected. Georgia didn't respond to Jenna's e-mail with the same friendly tone—in fact, she was downright nasty to Jenna. Even though Jenna had not accused Georgia of anything, the very fact that she wanted to change something Georgia had established set her off, and Jenna needed to find a way to make Georgia more reasonable about the situation. After several more back-and-forth e-mails, Jenna realized she wasn't getting through to Georgia, so she decided to call her.

Now that Georgia could hear her voice and tone, Jenna was able to communicate her concerns to Georgia. And Georgia, now putting a friendly voice to what she perceived as nasty notes, felt comfortable admitting to Jenna that she felt she was being attacked before they actually spoke to one another.

The two women enjoyed a friendly conversation, and Jenna was finally able to succinctly and tactfully let Georgia know what her concerns were, and address Georgia's trepidations in real time. Jenna pointed out that while the original playground had met all the requirements when it was installed, that safety regulations had changed in the past 10 years, and these new regulations should be incorporated into the design of a new playground.

Georgia could now process these concerns, without feeling attacked; she was also able to feel good about her past efforts, and what her future contributions could be. Jenna suggested that Georgia, a talented and well-regarded architect, could design the new playground, and Georgia accepted.

When the day of her meeting arrived, Jenna presented her case, and with several committee members (as well as the group leader) already aware of her agenda and how it would benefit them, the request to install a new playground was not only well-received, but unanimously accepted.

The Bearer of Bad News

Every now and again, the message you'll need to deliver will not be a popular one, and you'll need to find the most simple, direct way to get through to your audience—and quickly! This happened with one of our clients recently. Randall, the affable, approachable manager of a coffee packager/distributor plant, who was beloved by his employees, was at a loss on how to deliver some bad news to them.

The company was executing a highly visible, and potentially explosive, plan to close one of their two U.S. plants, in six months. In the meantime, they challenged each of the plants to work hard, with the promise that the "better" one would be chosen to remain open.

Each plant pulled out all the stops. Renouncing overtime pay, workers toiled on weekends, evening shifts, and even double shifts, to reach maximum productivity. Both achieved new productivity reports that were off the charts, though the northern plant was slightly higher overall.

At the end of six months, management announced that the northern plant would close. Lower taxes, lower wage scales, and cheaper shipping costs at the southern plant were cited as the reasons, though none of these factors had even been hinted at before.

Randall felt betrayed and angry. The plant was situated in a small town, where it had been the principle employer for decades, and he truly felt for his people.

Management had sent him a "talking paper" from which he was supposed to read, but how could he read cold, factual sentences that were full of phrases such as "outplacement counseling" and "severance packages"? What could he say that would make the blow any more acceptable?

I encouraged Randall to evaluate his relationship with his audience, and gave him a quick plan of attack.

5-MINUTE PLAN OF ATTACK

You aren't always given a lot of warning when bad news has to be delivered. While the powers-that-be know months in advance, they tend to keep that information close until they absolutely have to share it. So,,,, while you're processing the impact of decisions made, you'll also need to quickly find a sensitive way to deliver bad news. Here's a five-minute plan:

Minute 1: Decide how the disaster affects you personally, but then distance yourself from your own feelings.

Minute 2: Consider the position the people to whom you need to deliver the news may already be in, and how this news will affect that position.

Minute 3: Divide a piece of paper into two columns and list how the news affects you in one column and how it may affect them in the other.

Minute 4: Find a way to connect to their concerns—how are you going through this together?

Minute 5: Think of sincere ways you can offer your support, on which you can and will actually follow through.

Now take a deep breath and head out to break the news. Chances are, if you've really thought about how the news will affect others, and make that a pivotal part of your delivery, they may still, in fact, love you the next morning.

After weighing all of the information, he called his employees together on the production floor of the plant. He spoke to them from the heart—not as a corporate spokesman, but as leader of the team.

Speaking from the heart, he told them that they had fought as hard as they could, but that they had lost. He assured them he understood just how they felt: "I'm also frightened," he said, "because I, too, am out of a job."

Instead of being angry, the workers gave him a round of applause. He had captured their emotions while helping the group contain their rage and vent it appropriately. Then and only then did he move on to discuss severance packages and other details.

The Bottom Line

Whether you're in a situation like Andrea, who needed to coax her subordinates into going the extra mile without the extra reward; Jenna, a newcomer about to change old ways; or Randall, a usually likable leader who had to deliver crushing news without getting lynched, you have to know your audience, and what you can offer them, in order to get through to them.

In the next chapter, we'll get more into the specifics of tailoring a message to appeal to a particular audience, and uncover surefire tricks to get any audience behind you.

Probe: At a Glance

1. To whom do you need to speak?
2. How big is the audience?
3. What do you want from them?
4. What do they need to hear from you to give you what you want? (W.I.I.F.M.)
5. What can you offer to bring them over to your side?

Once you've established these parameters, and really gotten to know your audience, you're ready to head to the next chapter and learn how to position your message, so it has the greatest impact as possible.

STRATEGY 2

POSITION:
Massaging Messages and
Maneuvering Meetings

"The best way to predict the future is to invent it."
—Alan Kay, software inventor

Creating the future you want, and for our purposes, getting what you want from others, means orchestrating information in a way that not only appeals to them, but motivates them to act. You've already probed your listener. You already know exactly to whom you're talking and how you need to approach them. Now it's time to learn how to position your message, and organize the information you need to deliver in a way that is not only desirable, but digestible.

How you do this is the same for any size group whether it is an individual, an average-sized meeting, or a large presentation. Positioning is basic and easy to master, as I'll show you in this chapter.

As you plot your strategy, you must still keep in the back—okay, the front—of your mind, that most people are oversaturated, overwhelmed, and overwrought in our plugged-in world.

Work-life balance is out of whack across the board, and it's driving everyone nuts.

The good news is that the pendulum is starting to swing the other way. As Donna Ramer, president of Strategcations, comments, "There's an increasing trend toward setting more realistic deadlines. For example, many service and consulting companies have started to stand firm about not accepting unrealistic client deadlines, especially if they are last-minute-drop-everything-and-stay-up-all-night-to-get-it-done. There also seems to be more flexibility to establish deadlines both can live with, which may mean taking a few steps back to a time before overnight delivery and the immediacy of e-mail, a business-environment where the norm was to get things done correctly rather than quickly."

So, what does it mean to unplug? John Frazier, executive vice president of Quinn & Co. explains, "I sometimes impose a total news blackout on myself on weekends (if I can responsibly do it). That doesn't just mean no e-mail, it means no Sunday paper, no CNN, nothing. I don't do it every weekend, but when I can do it, I come back much saner on Monday morning." According to a recent article, Google engineers are encouraged to spend 20 percent of their time on some element of their work that they're passionate about, which is how Gmail, Google News, and Google shuttle buses (which bring employees to wok and back home again) were born (*New York Times*; October 21, 2007). But while the concept of not working like a machine all the time is starting to permeate the popular consciousness, the tendency to think of one's BlackBerry or cell phone as an appendage will likely get worse before it gets better.

Still, the distinction between living to work and having a balanced life is starting to be made. Statistics say:

- ⌑ Twenty-five percent of employees work in workplaces that offer flextime.
- ⌑ About 20 percent of employees occasionally work from home.

If ever it would be imperative to have a clearly crafted message, it's when you're in charge of a meeting. These days, meetings are out of control. Most people feel they attend too many, and never feel anything has been accomplished the entire time they're there—except that they've lost another hour or day of their lives, and are now further behind than ever.

It doesn't have to be like that. I'll show you how to take the reins of a meeting gone wild and tame it right back into submission.

In this chapter you will:

¤   Discover the flaws of the human memory and see how to make people remember you, despite everything else on their minds.

¤   Harness the power of your multitasking brain to develop a message map, your number-one positioning tool.

¤   Learn the smart way to plan and conduct a meeting, and learn to get these groups under control once and for all.

NOISE BLASTER!

Force yourself to take some semblance of a weekend—even if it's just for a half hour. If you want to be able to think straight during the week, unplug, recharge, and refocus.

Thoroughly Modern Memory

With all the commotion and clattering going on in the modern world, not only is it difficult for anyone to hear you, but when it comes to absorbing what it is you're saying, and then remembering it even an hour after you say it, well, you can forget about it. In this day and age, people are lucky if they remember to pick up milk or a pizza on their way home.

Of course we've all been there, and, as the lines between work time and time off remain blurred, it's only getting worse. How many times even this week have you made it to the top of the stairs, only to realize you have no idea what you needed in the first place?

One of the main problems is that people cram far too much information into a document or presentation, without providing any real focus or theme, hoping others will be able to grab a few nuggets of information by the time they're through. Unless you think strategically, and craft a message that will resonate hours, weeks, and months after you've delivered it, you may as well just talk to a wall.

What's in a Word?

How bad is human short-term memory? A lot worse than you may think. I see it every day in my workshops. In fact, in my seminars, I use a basic word game to prove just how tricky memory is. The outcome is always the same.

I start by telling the group that they're about to hear a list of 10 words regarding sleep. They're told they can write them down, but not until they've heard the last one. Then I list them: slumber, dream, insomnia, apnea, rest, evening, NyQuil, nightmare, wake, and REM.

I give them about a minute to write them down and then I ask them to tell me what's on their lists. It's rare that anyone ever gets them all. It seems like a light exercise, but it actually hits on several important elements of positioning a message:

⌺   Most people remember the first and last words. Invariably, almost everyone wrote down "slumber" (first on the list), and "REM" (last).

⌺   Most people remember words that have been repeated to them over and again—in this case, NyQuil (heavily advertised in the media).

⌺   Most people add something from their own brains when there are holes in what they remember or understand. In this case, most people added "sleep," which was not on the list. Why? When there is no context to the points being made, and there are too many points, people zone out because there is no "glue" holding the points together. Our brains are wired to process information at 800 words per minute; if there's nothing being said that keeps us connected, our brains will create our own material to have something to process.

So now that you know this, start to think about what's really going through someone else's brain when you're talking to them—and how much they're actually listening, absorbing, and understanding what you're saying. Scary.

Perhaps the scariest part of all is the part people make up for themselves when they don't hear or understand you, and the way the human brain will make the connections—instead constructing it's own version of what it *thinks* you're saying, which means that not only will the information a person takes away be severely distorted, it could be outright wrong.

Thanks for the Memories

The bad news is that science has not advanced to science fiction, in which a pill or procedure can guarantee the way the human brain digests and retains short-term and long-term information. The good news is, if you follow a few simple guidelines in crafting a message, you can at least improve the odds that some of what you say will be remembered.

⌺   Be sure what you say will land with the audience. Have you probed the psyche of this group to know what will persuade them?

⌺   Keep it simple. Life is complicated enough without you rattling off abstract concepts, unless your audience needs and desires them. Use nouns and verbs, but not a lot of adjectives.

⌺   Narrow down your bottom-line message to a few quick sentences of 12 to 15 words apiece. The larger the list of messages, the more likely it is that things will begin to fall off. Every presentation, whether you're making a point to one person or a group, should have a clear statement of your bottom line, and it should be mentioned early. And when it comes to informal presentations (such as an elevator or hallway) you could be cut off at any minute.

⌺   Jump right in. The first 30 seconds is everything, so you need a good grabber. Introduce the topic in a catchy, arresting, even amusing manner— maybe an anecdote, prop, or bottom line. Personal references break down barriers. Just avoid jokes, because they usually fall flat.

⌺   Remember the rule of first and last. People are most likely to remember the first and last things you tell them, so craft that opening and conclusion with care.

⌗ Repeat! Three is a magic number. Experienced and successful speakers, writers, and broadcasters all know that three words are better than one. There's a rhythm to speaking just as there is rhythm in music, and the rhythm coming from a sequence of three words is more likely to become implanted in the memory. If you're presenting a lot of facts in your presentation, it's a good idea to summarize your progress from time to time.

⌗ Draw it out for them. If you can help them visualize or create a mental picture of what you're saying for them, all the better.

⌗ Keep them involved. The more interactive the experience, whether you're building in Q & A or looking for active solutions for problem-solving, the more likely you are to keep their attention.

How the Other Half Thinks

In his best-seller, *A Whole New Mind: Why Right-Brainers Will Rule the Future*, Daniel Pink explains that, in the past several years, the world has been making a shift from linear thinking to what he calls a "Conceptual Age"—meaning that "big-picture" thinkers, those who embody "right-brain" qualities of inventiveness, empathy, joyfulness, and meaning—increasingly will determine who flourishes and who flounders.

What does this have to do with position messages for communication? The traditional way to build a core message and supporting arguments is to rely on the left-brain method, which relies on an outline with progressive sets and numbers. While that may be a great way to organize a party agenda or shopping list, broader core messages are more difficult to position, and rely on a different kind of thinking—one that's 360-degrees

TIPS FROM THE TRENCHES

Patreicia West

"When I'm about to present information to any size group, I try to make sure that I have simplified my design and message. This is especially important for me because of the way my brain works. I often see how ideas, concepts, and thoughts relate, link, and interface in sometimes unexpected ways, which requires what I call multi-layered thinking. I know others don't necessarily think this way, so I have to challenge myself to KISS (keep it short and simple).

"Sometimes, when there's a lot at stake, I'll script my conversation or message. I'll also make a lot of effort to find just the right word to convey my meaning. I find that this can make the difference in being 'on point' or having something lost in the translation—the difference between someone saying 'I understand' and 'I get it.'

"The scripting is to make sure that I have covered the most important points or have addressed the points in particular order. Sometimes after I've created a script, I'll put 'trigger words' on index cards and refer to them when I am actually in the conversation or delivering the information or message.

"I try not to ever memorize anything. It is too rote and it never comes across as 'being in the moment,' which is especially important in a conversation."

and three-dimensional, versus linear and one-dimensional. But before we get into the differences in these different types of thinking, let's take a quick look at what it means to be left-brained or right-brained.

Left-brainers are logic-driven, detail oriented, facts-focused, order-obsessed, practical, "math and science" types.

Right-brainers are intuition-driven, big -picture oriented, meaning-focused, imagination-obsessed, impetuous, "philosophy and religion" types.

Most people are focused one way or the other, but many can see both sides. At the time of this writing, a popular graphic on the Internet was that of a turning dancer. If you saw her turning clockwise, you were considered "right-brained"; counter-clockwise, and you'd be "left-brained." Many people could only see her turning in one direction or the other, but others, through sheer will, could see her change direction, which means that if you are typically a left-brainer, you can train your brain to see "right" for a while and follow the important positioning exercise I'm about to show you.

Message Mapping, which is a kind of contained brainstorming, is done not just by throwing words and phrases up onto a white board, but by actually encapsulating and structuring ideas as you have them, is a very "right-brain" way of doing things—with a nice "left-brain" structuring. It's kind of the best of both worlds.

Also known as "cluster thinking," Message Mapping allows you to look at your ideas, and anything that relates to them at a glance, whether it is on a sheet of paper, a wall chart, or blackboard. It's a way of thinking that encourages creativity, because not only are words involved, but also symbols, colors, and unusual formats.

Take page 66 to a photocopier, enlarge it, and make a lot of copies because this is a tool you will use again and again—in your professional life, in your personal life, and whenever

Message Map: Concept

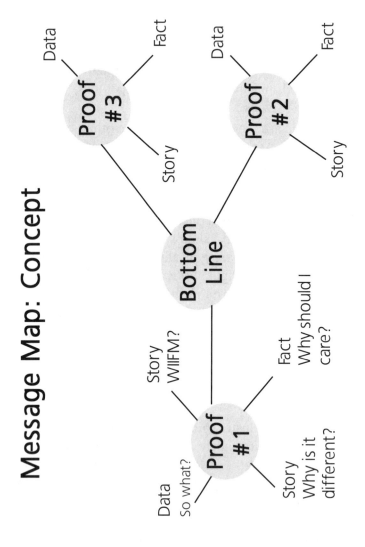

An example of a Message Map

you have a complicated message to deliver and need to map out what you want to say before you open your mouth.

The Message Map

Where do you want your listener or audience to end up once you've finished talking? What conclusion do you want them to draw? How do you want them to react to the information you've just presented to them? You can't build any kind of effective message until you answer these questions.

Start with the core message. That's the one right in the middle of the message map. Remember that a good core message can be summarized in a dozen words or so. It states the goal or outcome of what's being proposed in the plainest terms, and it focuses on the audience's needs, not yours. "Buy our tool. It offers exceptional accuracy at a lower price," or "Merging our companies will give us global reach, expand sales, and reduce costs," or "Vote for me. I can lower the debt without curtailing Medicare." If the core message is not that succinct, chances are your audience won't hear the rest of your message.

Write your core message in the middle circle of the message map. Now it's time for supporting arguments, which are the reasons, the data, the "proof" that persuades your listeners to act. These are the satellite circles. Ask yourself: "What else proves my core message? What does my listener, the jury in effect, need to hear to be persuaded to vote for me? What areas of resistance do I have to overcome?" As the scattered ideas grow in number around the message map's core message, inter-relationships begin to suggest themselves.

Say you have to give an actual presentation. A helpful guideline is to keep the points around the circle to no more than four. But as you'll notice on the template, you can also have supporting points to each of these satellite circles.

For a 20 minute presentation, you should have no more than four proof points on which to rely, so see what you have on your map and select them. For a longer lecture-type format, you could have as many as 10. Once the core statement and supporting arguments are worked out, the rest of your presentation will fall into place.

Message Mapping works equally well for half-hour presentations as they do for a 30-second selling opportunities at the water cooler or in the boss's office. And the whole organization process, incidentally, can be done in 15 minutes or less.

RABBIT TRICK: SAVING THE STEW

Direct marketing professionals John Graves and Dennis Lonergan, owners of Eidelon Communications, shared this Rabbit Trick, which demonstrates beautifully how having a firm handle on the core of your message and keeping your bottom line objective firm can help you salvage potentially unproductive meetings. In other words, too many cooks were spoiling the stew.

Problem: Eidolon Communications, a direct marketing firm in Manhattan with regional and national non-profit clients, was consistently presenting well-received creative concepts to one of its larger Washington-based clients. But while these concepts were being received with high lives of enthusiasm and excitement, few if any moved past the drawing board. The reason for this was that the clients loved participating in the creative process so much, they wound up shutting it down.

Solution: Eidolon took a new approach with the client, taking control of the terms and time frames of meetings, and did not allow ideas to sit on the table in an open-ended way.

"We would walk into a conference room with our boards and present them to our client, her boss, her staff, and other vendor partners on the account," says Dennis Lonergan, president of Eidolon. "Sometimes there would be more than 20 people in the room. There would be an initial rush of enthusiasm and excitement at our presentation, which often consisted of five to 10 unique ideas. People were energized and involved, but in a way that almost always led to the destruction of most of the ideas.

"After three or four presentations with the client, we learned to manage the process much more carefully. We reduced the number of ideas presented; identified the one we thought was strongest; anticipated reactions and possible 'suggestions' so that we were prepared to manage them decisively; and limited the duration of the presentation and number of attendees. Junior staff and vendor partners were no longer included; only our client manager and the two or three colleagues we knew she relied on to make decisions. Presentations were kept under 45 minutes, with the understanding that we had to leave promptly to make other appointments. As a result, discussion was far more focused and addressed only the ideas at hand."

By carefully managing the presentation of ideas, limiting the involvement of large and unwieldy groups, and ending meetings before an irreversible process of creative meddling takes off, they were able finally to get their great ideas greenlighted.

Take Control of Your Life, Please

A friend of mine, Lila, who is a Colorado-based freelance graphic designer and work-from-home mother of a toddler, was having a really hard time balancing work and home life (which is not unusual for people who work from home). That was the core of her problem. She not only *had* to work to help with the mortgage payments and put shoes on her little one who seemed to grow every week, she really *wanted* to work. When she had a creative outlet, she felt better about herself. Period. She was caught between two worlds, but there was no way she could choose one over the other.

However, the situation was wreaking havoc on her professional life, especially when it came to making her boss, Terry, understand what she was going through in order to get her work done. Lila felt as though Terry assumed she was too busy playing mom to take her work seriously; in actuality, Lila was putting so much of herself into her work, she barely had time for her family. She had to take charge of her life, and fast.

Lila told me she e-mailed her boss long status reports daily, and that still hadn't convinced the woman she was getting anything done. Terry simply replied that she didn't have time to read such lengthy e-mails! Lila drove an hour and a half once

NOISE BLASTER!

Write down everything that comes to mind when you brainstorm—even those points that seem unrelated at the time. It's amazing how often a random idea actually becomes the solution.

or twice a week to the company, and spent the day trying to look productive, even though most of her time was spent in pointless meetings and having her ear chewed off by a woman who sat in the next cubicle. Every time this other person came into her cubicle, uninvited, to talk about her kids, the boss invariably walked by.

I let the poor woman vent for about half an hour. I then told her to take a deep breath, and that I could help her not only to prioritize her deadlines and responsibilities and manage her stress level, I could also teach her how to communicate to her boss that she had things under control, and in her telecommuting situation, she was actually able to be more productive than she would have been at the office. The sigh of relief from the other end of the line was all I needed to get her started.

I first asked Lila to forward me some of her status e-mails, to see how she could be more succinct in reporting her daily activities to Terry. In every single e-mail, between explaining what she had been able to accomplish, were several apologies about not being able to get other things done. The ceiling sprung another leak. The baby was sick. The husband had tinkered with her computer to optimize her performance—and had shut her down for two solid days. Her babysitter quit. Her other babysitter had the flu. Her mother was too busy to watch little Dottie that week. All valid reasons to be behind the game—none valid for her boss's ears.

Lila said that the more she tried to communicate her concerns to Terry, the more distant she became. I told Lila that she first needed to stop making excuses. She needed to construct her status e-mails to focus on what was done, and, unless it was a deadline, to not even mention what hadn't gotten done. And above all, she had to keep the details of her work-from-home life back from her boss. I explained to her that if Terry worked at home or had a "well-meaning" husband or a "needy" toddler, she could certainly bond with her over these things. But because they lived in different worlds, what she was actually doing was alienating the other woman.

So why was Terry always calling for Sunday meetings? Why did she e-mail Lila in the evening when she knew that was Lila's family time? That was the other side of it. Lila said that the more she tries to work, to show her dedication to Terry, the more she feels she's wrecking her marriage by essentially ignoring her husband on nights and weekends, and scarring her daughter for life because Mommy never has time to play, no matter how much the little one begs.

Communication Clinic

I told Lila she needed to start setting boundaries with both her workplace and her home life. Instead of working sporadically around the clock, she needed to set a fixed schedule for work, and when it was family time, she needed to definitely pull the plug. Just because Terry wrote her e-mails at 10 p.m. didn't mean Lila had to answer them. And just because Lila was home during the day didn't mean she couldn't hire another babysitter, mother's helper, housekeeper, or some kind of help to make the household run smoothly while she was "at work."

I told Lila that, in order to properly communicate with her boss, she had to negotiate stronger guidelines, and stick to them. But first she had to communicate her needs in a language her boss would understand. She had to devise a clear, focused bottom line. To get there, I told her first to ask herself:

- ⌗   What is your contribution to the company?
- ⌗   What can you do to contribute to future growth?
- ⌗   Why are you so valuable?

I asked her to decide those unique strengths that made her a valued resource—so valued that she could negotiate the boundaries she desired. I also asked her to make a definitive list of what she was willing to give up, and what was non-negotiable.

The next step was to probe and analyze the situation regarding Terry.

- ¤   What are Terry's hot buttons?
- ¤   What is Terry's soft underbelly of business needs?
- ¤   Who at the company can Lila confide in, if anyone?
- ¤   Does Terry have a personal life or family?
- ¤   Where are the common bonds?

Status reports aren't book reports, so I told Lila that one thing she needed to work on was to streamline the messages she sent to the boss. She needed to make three or four points at the most, all factual, action-oriented, and "top-line":

- ¤   Is this project on track?
- ¤   What are the issues?
- ¤   Are you handling the issues? (Instead of diving into details, just give her a snapshot of your resolution to specific issues.)

I told Lila to think long and hard about the answers to these questions and then to arrange a face-to-face meeting with Terry, so they could talk it out in person. I explained Message Mapping and how it would help calm her down as she quickly drew her accomplishments and selling points on a piece of paper.

Centerpiece: I have ideas that can grow your company to the next level. (What business owner is not going to listen to this?)

Proof points:

- ¤   "I've grown X project into multiple projects for the company."
- ¤   "My dedication to the company against all odds has been proven time and again."
- ¤   "There are several opportunities to develop new seminar offerings, such as…"

⌑ "Here's where I can bend, and here's where I can't"—this is the "boundaries bubble."

The bottom line was that Lila needed to let her boss know that she was interested and enthusiastic about her work, and a valuable player in the company, even if she's not actually working "in the building." In order to be effective, she had to be able to objectively, substantively, and convincingly tell her why. For Lila, devising a message map with everything spelled out right in front of her was a great place to start.

TOUGH-LOVE TURNAROUND: THE DOORMAT

Do you really have work-life balance? Maybe you're watching someone else get constantly pulled into the hamster wheel of chronic and constant obligations. Whatever the case, if you don't get back in balance, if you don't learn to say no to your employer or even your family, you're going to burn out—with nothing to show for it—and what good is that?

You say: I've been working 24/7 for 10 years in this company and what has it gotten me? The corner office? No. A pot of gold? No. My boss doesn't appreciate me, and my coworkers take advantage of my good disposition. Worst of all, my kids have adopted the school bus driver as their parent. It's not *fair!*

I say: Stop whining and start acting. I know you've had it, your family knows you've had it, and your colleagues most likely know. But—and this is a big but—before you storm into your boss's office and bellow "No more!" as you hurl your company-issued BlackBerry at his thick head, take a breath.

You like your work and your coworkers, and your boss isn't so bad. It's the volume that's driving you nuts. You want to downsize the workload—and not get yourself downsized in the process.

So how do you reshape a job so that you'll still be valued, keep the prestige you've earned through all your hard work, and carve out some time for yourself?

Plan to have a meeting with your boss. Before you meet, pay close attention to the following:

- When is the best time to have the talk? You don't want to launch your position just before the launch of a new product.
- What time of day is he most approachable?
- What are his hot buttons?
- What's the talent pool like at the company?
- How is the work divided up in your department?
- Could you move to a different department (lateral moves are often desired nowadays to meet personal needs).
- By what percentage do you figure you need to reduce or redefine your load?
- Are there responsibilities you can take on while eliminating some of the more time-intensive tasks you're currently saddled with? One that may be easy for you to manage may be difficult for others. Say you're a creative type, but part of your job that eats up so much of your time is budget planning, and you're lousy at numbers. Could you share that position with a colleague? Are there tasks you could negotiate to take on?

As you're going over your points, keep your composure. Look at this as a negotiation. How will it help *the business* if you downsize your responsibilities? Remain focused on your bottom line, keep consistent with your points, and you'll soon arrive at some compromise. If not, it may be time to consider a new position at a new company.

Maximizing Your Message

In Lila's case, she essentially had points to make to one person: her boss, Terry. In that case, a simple Message Map worked wonders in not only cementing her bottom line, but also in addressing the variables attached to it. When you need to get information across to one person, you really could stop there. When you need to get more than one person on board with you, and everyone has different opinions about what the right course of action should be, it gets a bit more complicated. We'll get into this more when we look at meetings.

I worked with a client last year—let's call her Sally. Poor Sally had been promoted to a position to spearhead a new initiative. Implementing the new system would mean people's workloads would change—some would have heavier workloads, a few would have lighter ones, and, eventually, some people would have no jobs at all. Sally was now in charge of delivering messages to the staff and answering their questions as a point person. Or, as some like to call it, a target.

I worked with Sally to create what I call a Players Profile grid—essentially an at-a-glance look at who's involved, what side they're on, and what they have to bring to the table in terms of knowledge and interest. It's a different approach than the WIIFM grid we did earlier. That one specifically focuses on people's personalities and agendas; this one takes those into account against the backdrop of a specific situation (in this case, the new system).

For any situation, you'll have people for it, people against it, and people who couldn't care less. By pinning down exactly who knows what about what—and how everyone feels about it—you'll have, at a glance, a solid tool for seeing how to position your message to each individual for the most effective results.

From start to finish, the Players Profile Grid I developed with Sally took less than an hour to complete.

Name	Ally/Adversary/ Neutral	Level of Interest of This Initiative	Level of Knowledge for This Initiative
Nat			
Joe			
Paul			
Jean			
Marge			

NOISE BLASTER!

The best way to build consensus is to invite people to become part of the solution. As the project rolls along, continue to acknowledge the work people are doing. Spread success by publicly recognizing the contributions of everyone on the team.

Now, at a glance, Sally could see it all. She'd never mapped it out before, so she never truly knew who was against her and who could be on her side. Before, she was grasping at straws. Now she had a strategy.

When you use this chart yourself, and begin to analyze "players"—what their relationship is to you, the company, and so forth, you'll easily see with whom you need to align, who you should avoid, and who you may consider enlisting to help convert people you need to avoid yourself. (Just a note: many times, neutrals can be considered adversaries. It's not that they're against you, but they may not put forth the effort to help you either.)

Once Sally and I knew where everyone stood, we moved to the next strategy: bringing them over to Sally's side. Another quick chart and we had our answers again.

Mindset Modification Chart

Name	Anticipated Issues	How to Flip Them
Nat		
Joe		
Paul		
Jean		
Marge		

"One of the greatest handicaps is to fear a mistake. You have stopped yourself. You have to move freely into the arena, not just to wait for the perfect situation, the perfect moment. . . . If you have to make a mistake, it's better to make a mistake of action than one of inaction. If I had the opportunity again, I would take chances."
——Federico Fellini, director

5-MINUTE PLAN OF ATTACK:
LAST-MINUTE AGENDA CHANGE

Your boss just barged into your office in a panic, telling you some VIPs from headquarters are milling around, and that you need to quickly change the agenda of the meeting you've been preparing for the past week. It was supposed to be a meeting to discuss employee outings for that year, but your boss is worried that the higher-ups won't take your division seriously if they happen to slip into your meeting. You need to come up with an alternate plan—and fast!

Minute 1: Sketch out the framework for a Message Map on two separate sheets of paper—or, better yet, pull out two copies you have from the stack of blank Message Maps you keep at the ready in your top drawer.

Minute 2: In the core circle of each of the maps, write in a topic relevant to your division.

Minute 3: Consider the various proof points that could be included for each core topic.

Minute 4: Take a look at each and see which has the most proof points, and make that your topic.

Minute 5: Write the core message on the top of another sheet of paper, list three or four of the proof points underneath, and head to your meeting. Remember to also bring your Message Map for your own quick visual reference, and to use it when points come up that are not on your sheet.

While the one you chose may not be the best, it's the best under the circumstances. The topic with the most proof points is the one already more developed in your head, so you can use your Message Map as a guide.

Speak Up!

Recently, I coached an employee of a company I had just started to work with. I didn't know that much about the company—its dynamics, its politics—when I was signed on to coach Mary Beth.

Mary Beth was a frustrated, anxious mess. She was slated to present her strategy for a technology upgrade at an offsite corporate-wide meeting in two weeks. The trouble was, she was new at the company. Her colleagues didn't quite trust her because she was new to their industry and didn't quite grasp the lingo—the industry's or the company's. She didn't understand all the politics and dynamics, and when she tried to get preliminary feedback, her pleas seemed to fall on deaf ears. How could she competently present her plan without the feedback and information she so desperately needed?

Additionally she was unable to get support from her boss, who appeared to be distancing himself from the potential debacle.

Amazingly, this kind of situation is not unique. This kind of thing occurs everywhere nowadays. People are moving at a fast pace, and they can't get the attention of the decision-maker.

NOISE BLASTER!

When newcomers enter a project already in progress, take the time to bring them up to speed so they can understand the thought process that brought you to the point you're at. While an outside perspective may provide fresh insight, newbies need to know the history of the project, so their new ideas don't steer the campaign out of its parameters.

Perhaps they have been empowered to make decisions…until they make a mistake, such as going against the boss's unspoken, un-communicated vision. How could Mary Beth, or anyone in this situation, survive the presentation?

I advised her, as I now advise you, that there was no choice but to get the boss's attention long before The Big Meeting. But how?

I told her to think about the personality involved. The minute you're hired is the minute you need to start thinking about how you need to navigate the treacherous terrain of your new corporate environment, to find the path that leads to an open door from the one on top.

A strategy I recommend is to probe others about him. Align yourself with critical employees, business partners, or whoever has the ear of the person from which you need direction. You need answers to these questions (not that you'd ask these directly):

¤   Is the decision-maker bottom-line oriented?

¤   Is he a nuts-and-bolts thinker or high-concept thinker?

¤   Does he need to see the whole landscape to make his decision? And if he doesn't get it, will he automatically give a "no" response?

¤   Is he unfamiliar with your specialty—and perhaps uncomfortable admitting it?

¤   Is he…secure? Sincere? Strategic? Scattered? Selective (in hearing and in people)?

Find the answers to these questions and you'll see just how to approach him with a message—and how to position the message you need to deliver.

The following Meeting Mentor Questionnaire will help you to quickly assess what you're up against in getting your boss's attention. Writing down your analysis is important, because it will allow you to sit back and objectively analyze your thoughts as you get organized in your approach. Just be sure you keep this questionnaire private. It's definitely not a good idea to write it all over the white board in the conference room. But if you have to, be sure you thoroughly wipe down that board with glass cleaner, because you don't want any residue of the words to linger....

Meeting Mentor Questionnaire

Here's what the questionnaire should look similar to:

Personality

- Bottom line
- Literal, linear
- Scattered
- Impatient

Characteristics

- Cultural difference
- Language difference
- Age difference
- Works in same office as you?

Preferred method of communication

- Phone
- Face to face
- E-mail
- Other

Preferred scope of information

- A bit at a time
- Just the facts
- The whole enchilada

Opportunities to see the boss in person

- ⌑ Company event
- ⌑ Industry conference/trade show
- ⌑ Weekly, monthly meetings

Who has the boss's ear?

- ⌑ Administrative assistant
- ⌑ Project managers
- ⌑ Other

How can you get to him or her?

- ⌑ Forge a friendship
- ⌑ Offer to help out on a project
- ⌑ Other

Once you complete the questionnaire your plan of attack should pop right out.

Meetings, Miscommunication, Madness

"Why won't my people speak up when we're in meetings? They just sit there and look down at their notes or computers."

"Why does my boss do all the talking and run over my words when I'm trying to contribute?"

Both of these situations are so common in meetings these days, and they are a direct result of managers not directly communicating with their people, substantially strategizing before a meeting occurs. There's also the issue of subordinates not feeling comfortable asking their bosses for direction.

Every organization should designate at least one person in charge of telling people for what they are responsible in free-flowing meetings. In general, people assume too much, and, as a result, speak up too little or too much in meetings. Bosses assume that their team members will know what to say and when to say it. Employees assume that their bosses will

call on them in a meeting or tell them in advance if their participation is needed, or desired—or assume they have license to speak their mind at will.

It's amazing how many of us show up at meetings because we were required to be there, yet have no real sense of our purpose. It's time to get the purpose while you are in the planning stages.

Even if you don't have primary responsibility for a segment of a project—maybe you've been simply doing the research and analysis and handing it over to the leader—

you still need to step up when needed during any discussion of that project, and you need to do it in a way that doesn't discredit the person delivering the analysis to the executive committee or business partner.

Of course it's best if you, the principle presenter, and your boss (if she isn't already the principle presenter) can communicate in advance so you know who's supposed to say what—and also that everyone is on the same page with the facts and figures. But that's not always the case.

Sometimes you'll be called upon to support what the presenter is saying, but other times, you'll need to toss a life preserver to help that person if they're going off track or floundering. Some great "boss bail outs" include:

¤ "I remember the other day while working on the project I noticed…"

¤ "One other element we could consider might be…"

¤ "An unusual phenomenon I've noticed in this space is…"

Once you've made your entry, speak your correction as succinctly as possible and close your mouth.

Getting It Under Control

No matter what size your organization, no matter how many people you need to speak to, take a lesson from companies who have to present in high-visibility situations. During my career, I have coached hundreds of people to present or testify before regulatory agencies. This high-risk, high-reward opportunity calls for extraordinary preparation and discipline, and no detail is too small to overlook. When the time comes to present or testify, the day of The Big Meeting, everyone knows what is expected of him or her, thanks to layers of rehearsals.

Of course, not all meetings demand a strict and formal approach, but the discipline and "want no surprises" attitude of these operations will hold you in good stead. It will ultimately save hours of time, buckets of stress, and piggybanks of money.

If you can't get formal direction on how to conduct a meeting, find a way to ask your boss what the expectations are. If you're a new hire or a recent college graduate with limited experience you're actually expected not to know. But you were hired for a reason, and you need to make your voice heard in meetings. In all my 25 years of executive coaching, I've never once heard one supervisor say to me, "I sure hope those kids don't say anything in the meeting." On the contrary, they want you to speak up and say smart things because it not only reflects well on them, it shows team unity to clients and senior executives.

How do you approach your boss? You can start by approaching him or her like a human being. Stop by his office and ask: "Do you have two minutes? I have a quick question about The Big Meeting." If he needs you to come back at another time when he's less busy, he'll let you know. If he invites you in, take a deep breath and say something along the lines of: "I know you will be presenting the data, but I'll be happy to answer questions about details since I've been involved in the minutiae. How would you like me to do that? Should I wait until you call upon me or inject as I see appropriate?" In that way, you'll express interest in wanting to speak up as well as a line of support should he need to call on it. If your boss is chronically on the road, send a brief—and I mean *brief*—e-mail with just enough for him to read with one click.

In my experience, the best presentations are shared experiences where everyone at the meeting has a role.

Keep Them Happy

Everyone wants to feel wanted. So, while we want to be paid for doing our job, we also need to be rewarded with words. We want to know we're doing a good job.

We all need a pat on the back as much as we need a paycheck. Having a one-on-one conversation with an employee is a great way to offset griping. Maybe your staff needs to work late, and won't be compensated for it; make them feel valued in other ways. Try something such as, "I have never been so proud of a team before," and then say something positive about each member of the group. When you validate, encourage, and stimulate morale, you'll change the tonal center of the meeting and move into the positive realm.

Another way to set a good tone for a meeting is to bring something special. Treats such as cookies or candy make people happy. Flowers are a bright touch, too. If it's after hours, you can turn it into a party with a little wine and cheese to ease the thought of another late night at the office.

If you're going to preempt problems in a meeting, bring in some fun with you. What are people doing to lighten it up in this age of turbulence? If a meeting starts at 7 a.m., maybe the boss brings in Krispy Kremes. This gesture makes attendees happy. Maybe it's the thought that matters; maybe it's the sugar rush. Whatever it is, it works.

Say you're a factory foreman and you're forced to hold mandatory Friday afternoon meetings and everyone hates you for it—especially in the summer time. So maybe once a month, tape a goody under one of the chairs—something that won't cost a lot, but that the staff values.

Sometimes if you just take the time to shake things up a little once in a while, you'll energize your people and lessen the likelihood that they'll disrupt your meetings.

One woman I know once brought in rubber snakes to a meeting to get her people's attention. Maybe you're all trying to get through a project you hate, or you're strategizing how to work with a client who continually tortures you. Commiserate with your people by bringing in something that shows you understand the hell they're going through, such as a devil's food cake. A gesture like this not only relieves tension, it strengthens support and allegiances. It gives us a chance to laugh, and laughter is the best tension reliever I know.

Maximize Your Meetings

Here are some quick tips for facilitating your next meeting:

⌑ For a large meeting (a small meeting will always be less formalized), send out an agenda beforehand, outlining not only what will be covered, point by point, minute by minute, but also any ground rules (no BlackBerrys, and so forth.)

⌑ Have meetings with individuals before the meeting as a way to gage who will be for you and who will be against you. Here are some good grabbers: "I want to make this meeting worth your while," and "What would you like to see incorporated into the agenda?"

⌑ The opening statement sets the tone for the meeting, so have a strong one ready.

⌑ Try to engage everyone present, whether by citing achievements or areas of expertise, or simply directing questions to specific participants. Steve Kyler, director of IT Solutions, AVI, specifically says, "Attention spans are limited. Try not to go on for more than 10 minutes without having questions or other types of audience interaction."

⌑ Avoid yes or no questions, and instead, pose questions that will open a discussion. Instead of "Would this work?" ask "How would this work?"

◻ Watch the clock. No one likes a meeting to run over—especially into another meeting. You'll lose people's attention if they feel like you're not paying attention to the time—they'll gladly do it for you, at the expense of listening to anything .

◻ Close your mouth. If you're facilitating the meeting, you should be talking 20 percent of the time; your participants should be talking 80 percent.

◻ Get the key objectives out there right away in case people try to slip out early.

◻ As you get to the end, inquire as to whether or not participants found the meeting useful—why and why not—then quickly summarize and wrap up.

A Crisis for Christopher

A sales manager was preparing for the company's national sales meeting, trying to anticipate questions that might pop up from the sales force. He figured they would be asking the obvious—margins/commissions, territory shifts, and so on. What he didn't anticipate was the CEO changing course in the middle of the discussion.

Out of nowhere, the CEO jumped up and announced there was going to be an acquisition that would fundamentally alter the strategy of the sales force. Once he made this announcement, the CEO picked up his coffee cup and left the room.

Our sales manager, Christopher, was frozen. Here he had taken all this time to plan a meeting to boost his people and motivate them to sell, and the CEO came in and dropped an atom bomb on the proceedings. He was at a total loss, his mouth a gaping hole.

After taking a deep breath, he called for a 15-minute break to restrategize his presentation, and returned to his desk. There, he came up with a Plan B.

5-MINUTE PLAN OF ATTACK: BAD NEWS BOMBSHELL

It happened to Christopher. It could happen to you: Right in the middle of your meeting, someone will say something to sink your original message like a cinderblock to the bottom of the sea. How can you quickly get things back under control? How did he?

Minute 1: Christopher returned to his office, closed the door, and took a deep breath to gain his composure.

Minute 2: He took out his original Message Map for this meeting and analyzed which parts of it were still usable.

Minute 3: He located a meeting priority point, and, on a fresh message map, made it the core.

Minute 4: He branched out new priority points and began to see a way to keep the meeting productive as well as cathartic.

Minute 5: He grabbed his Message Map and headed back to the conference room, where he rehearsed points in his head, visualizing his people back in their seats, as he awaited their return.

You always want to have a contingency plan, but just in case you don't, your Message Map can become your parachute.

When he returned, he allowed his people a 30-minute venting period. He took in everything they were saying about lay-offs, salary freezes, territory shifts, and more traveling than they already did. He listed their concerns on a chart to let them

NOISE BLASTER!

If you're working with a particularly volatile group, or you're aware in advance of bad news coming, factor in a little time for people to grouse and gripe before you present.

know their comments were being heard and considered. Obviously, he had no answers then and there, but once he got the list of the main concerns, he turned the boss-bashing into a brainstorming, asking his people to consider what they all knew about the acquisition and to rethink their sales strategy from there.

The moral of the story is to always think beyond the obvious—to listen to rumors (as remote as they may be), as well as to customer complaints, actions by competitors, vendors, and joint venture partners.

**RABBIT TRICK:
SAVING YOUR IDEAS**

Problem: You need to develop a creative campaign for a new client, but all your ideas are getting rejected by the head of marketing. The trouble is, you're not getting any feedback or specific direction. All that happens is your piece is returned to you, by an assistant, with a big red "no" scrawled across the top. You have no idea what about your effort is working and what isn't. What do you do?

Solution: It's time to call a meeting. This person needs to communicate his of her specific needs in front of you and others, and make a commitment to you about what he or she specifically wants—and to stop wasting your time. Easier said than done, right? Ask around. See how other people have handled this situation with this person. Speak to your boss about helping to get a meeting arranged. The longer he or she continues to operate like this, the more time and money is being wasted. Especially if your boss is someone who has a vested stake in the financial health of the company, will he or she align with you to get what you need?

As Cabot Parsons of Parsons James Brand Architecture advises, "If you don't have the ultimate decision-makers in the room at the beginning, your chances of an effective consensus are next to none. Make it a point to insist that the person with the ability to greenlight a campaign approach is present during all of the first stages, rather than waiting to be approached at the end of the process. If the boss has heard all of the discussion of the issue at hand, and participated in defining what a successful solution would be, then once that solution is developed, his/her support will be there as the solution is implemented.

Face to Face, or Interface?

Lester Davis, president of Basilio Advantage, says, "There used to be an urgency to use every piece of e-technology available—e-mail, virtual meetings, Web conferences, and so forth—as these were perceived to make meetings and communications more efficient. But as people have become ever-more exhausted by the options available for not actually being in the same room with others, the opposite seems to be true. More and more, people are turning towards in-person, face-to-face meetings that are smaller, interactive, and more focused."

NOISE BLASTER!

"For meetings, live is always best, but as technology becomes more sophisticated, video conferencing is a good alternative," says Steve Kyler, director of IT Solutions, AVI, Inc.

Teleconferencing works best when a project is already up and running, and all the key participants have all previously met in person. When a new project is being launched, or when a new member comes into the group, you need the energy, the face-time, and team-building that an in-person meeting provides.

TIPS FROM THE TRENCHES

Merril B. Corry
vice president, Logistic Innovations
The most significant trend has been the use of technology to create and share messages with a shared audience. This factors into the attendee's preference to stay closer to home and family, and partake in the virtual world. It also is a direct effect of companies' ever-tightening budgets within marketing plans to increase the number of people who will benefit from the message.

In meetings, whether digital or live, people favor peer interaction. People value their colleagues' input and like this format and learning style. They'll be much more apt to attend a meeting conducted in this fashion, and will feel their participation and valued time have been put to good use as they have not only gained knowledge, but provided it.

Please, Not Another Meeting!

Who hasn't complained that there are just too many meetings and that they last too long? You'll be a hero if you're known for keeping your meetings as infrequent as possible. So, before you schedule the next meeting...

⌑ really think about whether getting together in person is really essential—or if there might be another efficient and effective way to get your particular project off the ground. Frankly, any creative venture needs face time and the electricity of great minds working together, so the first meeting is critical, as is a milestone meeting. Others can be done through video conferencing and conference calls.

⌑ decide whether everyone has to be there. Figure out who really needs to be involved. Generally speaking, the power people—the key players— need to be there, but some meetings designed to "build consensus," with no decision-making objective, are usually time-wasters.

⌷   determine whether a key person who can't be there in person, can be patched in either by phone or videoconferencing. Video conferences, in which teams of people or virtually all of the players are separated physically, are proliferating as a method of holding meetings. Of course, they come with their own share of headaches if there are transmission glitches.

⌷   see if you can give people a preview? Preparing a long agenda and circulating it ahead of time can actually make for a shorter meeting, because a well-crafted agenda can establish the specific parameters of the discussion, prevent time-wasting digressions, and show who's in charge from the outset.

⌷   Too many meetings start with housekeeping details—the rules of discourse, when breaks are scheduled, and extended introductions. Housekeeping details should go into your pre-circulated agenda, so that you can get right to the meat of your meeting. Grab them in the beginning, you'll hold them for the day.

The Bottom Line

How you position the information you will be delivering is as important as the information itself, whether you're giving a conference to a large group or meeting face-to-face with your boss or subordinate. Getting a sense of who they are and what they need to hear from you comes first; taking these elements into account is essential to how you position that information. Which points you emphasize and which you downplay as you deliver your message can make all the difference in how it is received.

When you have a meeting, lay down the law. Not having ground rules for meetings leads to bad behaviors. People can basically review their BlackBerry, have side conversations, arrive late, or come and go as they please. When clear meeting ground rules are posted, attendees realize what's expected from them, and distractions (such as coming in late, side discussions, reading, paper shuffling, cell phone and BlackBerry usage), will not be permitted.

Position: At a Glance

1. How will you grab your listener?
2. What is your bottom line?
3. Have you completed your Message Map?
4. Have you plotted your time realistically?
5. Do you have a strong bottom line?

Now that you know how to position what you want to say, to an audience you've taken the time to know, it's time to learn how to present yourself in a way that will make people trust, regard, and like you, and want to listen to you and act on what you say. So in the next chapter, it's time to learn the finer points of *persuasion*.

STRATEGY 3

PERSUADE: Mastering the Corner- stones of Persuasive Communication

"Your pitch is like live TV—there's no room for error."
—Michael Platt, president of Design Write

A tall man who looks like he may have once played football, Michael Platt quietly enters the room. A warm look on his face, he nods a cordial hello to colleagues and takes a seat on the side of the large boardroom table, not at the head, which is unusual because this man is the boss.

Everyone in the room is aware of his energy, and he has yet to open his mouth. As others enter, he remains cordial yet quiet. His presence, however, fills the room.

As the meeting commences, he listens. He watches the body language around the table. And just when you think he's there merely as an observer, he asks a penetrating question that, in a nutshell, sums up all the unspoken issues that have been floating about the room. He then gently guides the discussion to where his team believes the endpoint needs to be.

Within the first 30 minutes of this meeting, Platt exhibited the four aspects of persuasion:

1. **Chemistry.** He positively impacted his team without even opening his mouth. Where he chose to sit showed solidarity; nodding or smiling to everyone as they came in showed that he acknowledged them as important members of his team.

2. **Clarity.** He carefully listened to what was actually going on before finding a solution for his staff. He didn't just trumpet his own agenda all over them without knowing from where they were coming.

3. **Credibility.** He had done his research on the issue, and he was ready for the tough questions.

4. **Consistency.** Michael can be counted on to display the appropriate business behavior. People around him become calmer and more focused because of his approach to handling his people's needs.

What makes people, like Michael, unique is that they have figured out enough to project their personalities without saying a word, and are also well aware of the personalities around them.

To be persuasive, it's essential to be able to see yourself through the eyes of others. Platt knows he can be imposing, so he plays it subtle. The point is that, if you take the time and effort to analyze your strengths and weaknesses, and pay attention to the strengths and weaknesses of others—to play off the strengths and work around the weaknesses, and not the other way around—you will have a room eating out of your hand.

When persuasion works, it really works, and someone who masters the nuances of persuasion can become a leader. Born or made, being a leader has everything to do with charisma, knowledge, and focus. That absolutely does not mean you need to become a slick, fast-talking huckster type; you simply need to have a conscious awareness of your underlying goals and your audience, and deliver a message with focus. In this chapter, you will:

- discover the cornerstones of persuasion and why each is essential to master.
- learn the pluses and pitfalls of email.
- see why listening can be as important as speaking.
- find when to be yourself and when to adapt to suit a situation.

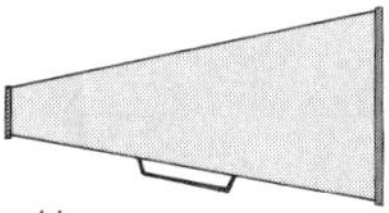

NOISE BLASTER!

It only takes 30 seconds for someone to size you up. In addition to making sure your appearance is impeccable, be sure the first thing that comes out of your mouth really makes a difference.

Better Living Through Chemistry

"Do they like you?" It seems so very high school, yes, but persuasive communication absolutely depends on it. Not entirely, but initially.

To be persuasive, first and foremost you must make a positive personal impression on your audience. Individual or group, it doesn't matter—your message is only as good as the personal impression you make. People make a snap decision about you the minute you walk into a room by how you seem to them or how you shake their hands. Are you thinking and feeling in the present? Are you there when you walk into a room? They will know immediately, as you do. Do you want to be around that person or not?

Some elements of chemistry will be out of your control—and that can be both good and bad. Are you lucky enough to have an already established good rapport? If you remind your listener of someone they like, you're off to a great start. But, unfortunately, just as positive associations can help you, negative ones can hurt. If your appearance and manner remind someone in your audience of a person he or she doesn't like or trust, you have an uphill battle from the beginning. It's going to be very hard for you to win them right off the bat. Luckily, there are ways you can override a preconceived notion someone has of you.

Of course, you can't get a makeover while you're speaking, but there are ways to alter the way you come across to others, and pretty easily. It could be as simple as adjusting your delivery. Look to your listener for clues to help you tweak your method of delivery and make a "chemical" connection. Pay attention to his or her speech patterns—is the person prone to words that are visual, auditory, kinesthetic? Pay attention to their patterns and preferences, and mirror them in your own speech. When a person senses you are "like them," they'll be more open to establishing a rapport with you.

Just be sure you always keep positive. Avoid picking up questioners' negative language or tone of voice. Even when delivering bad news, you will want to offset it with a strategy

NOISE BLASTER!

For decades, Art Stevens owned an award-winning international Public Relations agency. He was responsible for public relations programs for Fortune 500 clients and managed hundreds of account executives and creative directors. Art believes that solid, direct communication is at the core of his life-long success.

His approach to ensuring that communication was on the right course for his team he would lead role-playing exercises during brainstorming sessions. During these sessions, team members would play the role of the client and also play the role of fellow team members. "These role playing demonstrations not only stimulated the creative juices, reports Stevens, they became bonding exercises for team members.

The bottom line is that we were designing unique and edgy PR campaigns and retaining talent because the team became closer and more productive.

to reverse the trend. Take for example, the hypothetical question, "Isn't it true that unconventional competition is hurting the business?" You may find yourself using use the questioner's negative word *hurting* in your answer, but that will only reinforce that negative premise through repetition. Try instead, "I wouldn't refer to it that way. What I would say is…" and then use your own words. This will help keep you in control. We'll talk more about how to reverse these situations in our last strategy, *preempt*.

For getting buy-in from your staff, your boss, and your colleagues, chemistry is absolutely essential. Do they want to be with you? Do you threaten them? Especially in recent years, employers have been more open to admitting that they are more apt to hire a person they like, over a person who may be more qualified, but less affable.

NOISE BLASTER!

More than 90 percent of what people take from a presentation is impression—which includes vocal tone, mannerisms, and command presence. Maintaining eye contact is essential, as are natural gestures that help to burn off nervous energy.

Chemistry Chameleon

While it's essential for you *to be yourself* to deliver a genuine message, there are times you may need to get "around" yourself a bit—to modify your personality to match the chemistry of "the room" (a term I use to mean the conference hall, the conference room, or the cubicle).

Is your personality too big? Could you take it down a notch? Is it too small or subtle? Do you need an energy infusion? Are you going to get lost in the crowd—even though you're supposed to be leading it? How can you adapt yourself to various settings to persuade effectively? If you're meeting with a linear-thinking person who is threatened by big, personal movements, he will shut down if you start gesticulating wildly. If you are naturally gregarious, avoid your natural tendency toward "touchy" and "feely." Are you shy? Someone may interpret your reluctance to open up or be touched in any way as being ineffectual. Plan something to say, and say it as soon as you can squeeze it in. Take a breath. Relax. Let go for a while and let the other version of you take the lead.

If you've ever met me in person, you know I'm no shrinking violet. Terms people use to describe me include "force of nature," "whirlwind," and "stream-of-conscious thinker." Yet, many of my clients are very conservative, high-level corporate executives, would probably get on the phone to the mental hospital within minutes if I ever stepped out of "business" character during meetings. You do what you have to do.

If you are trying to persuade someone with very different background, no vested interest in helping you—you better come up with a way to bond with them.

NOISE BLASTER!

Whether you're talking to one or 1,000, small room or big, keep your tone conversational. Let your personality and passion come through your words. Keep your mind focused on the words, and the meaning behind the words, as you speak them and you'll be surprised how this will convey your passion for your subject.

Bullying Backfires

A rotten personality can tip any apple cart. God knows it happens every day in every office. One cranky person spoils the mood and drags everyone else down.

I'm reminded of a meeting I was overseeing for a designer and manufacturer of athletic shoes. The entire team involved in creating the sneakers and building publicity for the product were all called together in a room just before the launch. They thought they had been summoned there for a pep talk, maybe even a pat on the back from the CEO, who had called the meeting. They were excited to have this open forum with him, and were poised and ready with questions and comments for an open discussion about the product and the future.

The CEO came into the meeting 15 minutes late, and in a foul mood. He walked to the front of the room and got everyone's attention by loudly clearing his throat. "There's a lot of money riding on this product," he said gruffly, "and the future of this company rests on your shoulders. You better not screw it up." It doesn't take a rocket scientist to know that his subsequent request for questions was greeted by dead silence and a look of stunned agitation on people's faces. It seems extreme, yes, but these kinds of things happen every day in meetings. The leader comes in, sets an uncomfortable tone, and the meeting implodes.

This CEO was acting like a dictator. He thought he was stimulating a call to action, but what he thought was coming across as passion was interpreted as threats.

The lesson to be learned here? Maybe try not screaming at your people. Take a lesson from the probing chapter, and get to know them. Bond with them. The cranky CEO could have made his people feel valued over their efforts, and still gotten his message across about how much was riding on this particular account.

Learn your people's personalities. Tell them what they *need* to hear in the way they need to hear it. We all like to think of ourselves as persuasive people, but if you intimidate people to get their work done, are you really persuading them to stay with you through thick and thin? How's the morale over there at your place? Remember: hysteria is not persuasion. Coercion is not persuasion. Bonding is persuasion.

5-MINUTE PLAN OF ATTACK

You're sitting at your desk. Your office has a casual dress code, so you're wearing khakis and a button-down shirt. Logging on has been slow today, and you're waiting for your e-mail screen to come up as you sip your coffee and nibble your muffin. Then the phone rings. It's the head of HR.

"Didn't you get my e-mails?" she asks, panicked. You explain about the server and she speaks right over you. "I'm heading to the job fair at the University. Jay was supposed to come with me, but his kid's sick and now I'm stuck. I know I recruited you from that school, so I need you to come down and join me. I'm on my way. Meet me there in 20 minutes!"

Now what? It will take you about 10 to 15 minutes to get to the school, depending on traffic, so take five minutes to prepare.

Minute 1: You always keep a sports jacket and tie (or if you're a woman, a pair of plain pumps and a neutral jacket) in your office, so first get yourself spruced up.

Minute 2: Next, whip out a pen and paper and take some notes. First pin down the mission statement of the company. Find out who's taking the lead and what the general themes are.

Minute 3: Think back and remember the story of how you were recruited by ABC Corp.

Minute 4: Think of the three reasons that make ABC Corp. more innovative, employee sensitive, and enjoyable (or anything else that will be attractive to a perspective employee), than their competitors.

Minute 5: Think of some of the ways you can persuade a good candidate to give ABC Corp. a serious second look. What specifically can ABC Corp. offer "you" (your listener, the potential recruit).

Now take your notes and head out. Good luck!

NOISE BLASTER!

A written sentence can be 25 words long, but spoken out loud; sentences should be around 10 words. Shorter sentences not only allow for better breathing on your part and help you maintain your energy level, they're also easier for listeners to quickly grasp.

Clarity Is Key

If you're not clear about what you're saying, it doesn't matter how much an audience likes you. They may like listening to your voice and being in your presence, but how are you going to get them to act on your behalf if they have no idea what your behalf actually happens to be?

As you're speaking, step away from yourself. Look for signs. Does this person or group really understand you, or are they just being polite? Sometimes people will pretend to listen to you, so eventually you will finish up what you're saying and go away.

Does it seem like your audience has any sense of the subject matter? It's a sad fact of life, but especially in a professional setting, a confused listener will almost always pretend to know what you're talking about, rather than have you explain it. No one wants to look like the "group dummy," so if no one else is asking questions, a person may just assume he or she is the only one not getting it.

Do you speak the same language? By this I mean figuratively and literally. Do you speak the same technical language? Are you talking computer technology to a group of former English majors? Are you discussing Proust to a room full of linear-minded techies? Go back to *Probe*. Get familiar with

TIPS FROM THE TRENCHES

Michael Platt, president of Design Write

"Our clients are our 'backbone,' so it's essential to keep our communications with them clear and our relationships strong. Service is everything.

Before meeting with a new client, I always encourage my people to Google and find out exactly who's going to be in the room with us.

We prepare for meetings as a team. We evaluate with whom we will be meeting, and we take into account which of our people will best relate to members of the client team. If we're going to do a large pitch, I read the room first. I listen to people as they come in. Then, I think about the personalities on my team and strategize where they should sit.

Once we develop a relationship, I encourage my staff to:

⌑ be consistent by having daily contact with customers to cement relationships and keep in tune with what their needs.

⌑ be credible and stay abreast of industry issues. How can you exhibit credibility if you're asking your customers for trends? You should stay on top of these in order to offer advice and solutions. Speak with integrity.

⌑ be clear in both speaking and listening. Listen to the agenda—actual and hidden—and ask appropriate questions when something hasn't been made clear."

the people to whom you're talking and find out how to best explain what you're saying.

Industry buzzwords aside, we're an international culture now, and language conventions such as idioms get lost and misconstrued all the time. Learn the keys to another's culture. Is it important to ask about the family beforehand? The Japanese take an hour just sitting and getting comfortable with the dynamics of the meeting. They're used to sizing up people first, not just jumping in, as Americans are more apt to do.

People are not going to help you get what they want if they're zoned out. You have to blend in with them and bond. Do your homework. If you're speaking to a group from another culture, read up on it.

Mystery Words

When you speak and write, avoid using any of these words and phrases, and ones like them, as they are not concrete and only promote confusion:

¤ "In a timely manner." Does that mean immediately? Next week? If it's up for interpretation, it could mean in the next century for all anyone knows.

¤ "Just now." In some regions, this means literally "just now"; in others, it could mean sometime in the next hour, day, or week.

¤ "I'll be there in a minute." Really? In exactly 60 seconds? Because that's what a minute is—not 15 minutes, not an hour.

¤ "I'll see you later." When later? In a few minutes? Next year? How long should this person wait for you?

And if you're getting too many mystery words from someone trying to tell you something, speak up if you don't know exactly what's being asked of you.

What Works?

I can tell you what *doesn't* work: talking over someone's head. That means you're peppering your message with too many colloquialisms or jargon, or any terminology that isn't readily accessible.

You also want to use strong, active, positive words. Speak in an active voice, not a passive one. Not "I am convinced by the research," but "The research convinces me." Use nouns and verbs—and as I mentioned earlier, be conservative with the adjectives. The words hit right where you want them to: in the heart, the stomach, the wallet. Instead of saying something bland and colorless, such as: "I think this proposal should be approved," you must be substantive. Add feeling, and start strong: "The research really convinces me that this proposal should be accepted…" and then provide solid examples as to why.

TIPS FROM THE TRENCHES

Cabot Parsons
Parsons James Brand Architecture

"There's much less of a mass market than there was even five years ago, which means there is much less of a mass mentality. We don't actually all have the same background experiences, priorities, and beliefs these days. This makes mindful listening and asking questions a much more effective and productive way to exchange ideas than simply making assertions. The old adage, 'seek first to understand, then to be understood' is more relevant today than ever."

Listening Skills

Just as it takes two to tango, it takes two to communicate. Far too many people talk and don't listen. Listening is a concentration. Focus on the person talking to you. Not only will you be able to pick up a lot more than you would normally, you'll also be increasing the bonding messages your body language is sending:

⌘ Don't stand so close. If you invade another person's comfort zone, you're going to make them nervous, and as a result, they'll be more focused on creating distance from you than actually listening to what you're saying.

⊐ Keep asking questions based on the answers the person with whom you're speaking provides. For example, if you ask a person what she thinks are the most important elements of her job, and she veers off into the realm of ways she could do better if she had more staff, bring back the elements that are important, and direct her to spell out why each of these functions could be improved with more help.

⊐ Maintain eye contact. How much faith do you have in a person who, while you're talking, appears to be reading something on the ceiling?

TIPS FROM THE TRENCHES

Jack Cloonan
president of Clayton Consultants

"In my prior line of work as an FBI agent, it was absolutely essential for me to recall details of meetings I had with people through the years. Often times, I found myself in situations where I was not able to take any notes. So, how did I remember what was said and what wasn't? What was pertinent and what was superfluous? How many details of a conversation might be lost in a manner of hours? I developed a simple strategy to jog my memory and that was 'visualization.'

"Essentially, I'd recreate the entire meeting or interview in my mind by using a mental time line. For example, where was the interview? If it was a restaurant, then, I start to recall where I sat, what the interviewee was wearing, which helped me reconstruct the discussion. As I started to visualize the setting, details of the conversation began to emerge. As I began to make notes based on the visualization exercise more and more specific details flowed into my consciousness. It worked for me."

Listening Signal Words

It doesn't matter how powerful a speaker you are, you have to face the fact that people's attention wanders. You can do that with trigger phrases that will bring your listener back to you. Remember school? Every teacher's favorite was probably "This will be on the test." Here are some more to keep in your arsenal:

- ¤ "What's significant here…"
- ¤ "I want to stress…"
- ¤ "Let me underscore…"
- ¤ "What's important here…"
- ¤ "This is the key message…"
- ¤ "In conclusion…"
- ¤ "If you remember nothing else, remember this…"
- ¤ "To summarize…"
- ¤ "Let's review"

E-mail: Clarity Killer?

In an article called "E-Mail is Easy to Write (and to Misread)," Dan Goleman told a story about an e-mail exchange he was having with a person who worked at the publishing company that was putting out his most recent book. They were haggling over "some crucial detail involving publishing rights." He thought the exchange was going well. She did not, and sent him an e-mail saying: "It's difficult to have this conversation by e-mail. I sound strident and you sound exasperated." It was not how he saw it at all. He writes: "I was surprised to hear I had sounded exasperated. But once she identified this snag in our communications, I realized that something had really been off. So we had a phone call that cleared everything up in a few minutes, ending on a friendly note."

E-mail. It can be a communications catalyst. It can also a colossal catastrophe. The problem with e-mail is that if you want it to be the former, you have to use it correctly. If you abuse it, not only are you not going to get your point across, you're going to alienate others instead of bonding with them.

NOISE BLASTER!

We speak 125 to 144 words a minute, but the average typing speed is only about 60 words per minute. If someone's taking notes on what you're saying, that means more than 50 percent of your message will probably be lost. Pausing and speaking deliberately will give your listener more time to absorb what you're saying.

Take, for example, this classic scenario from a writer friend of mine. She was trying to focus on a hugely important deadline, but had to keep her e-mail activated because she was waiting for a crucial piece of information to wrap her story. It was supposed to get sent to her that day. She kept the "beep" on her e-mail so she could step away from her computer and focus on her work; she could work across the room on her laptop and only get interrupted when the beep sounded.

When the beep sounded earlier than expected, she thought: Hooray! She could finally finish; the piece of information she was waiting for would finally move the project along! When she checked the screen, she saw it wasn't what she had expected, but instead, an e-mail from a former associate who had just gotten a new cat. Great. Good news is always a welcome distraction. And it didn't really faze her when she saw there were about 25 other people listed in the "to" list. Not yet anyway.

Within minutes, however, those 24 other people would become the bane of her very existence when everyone began responding.

They wrote about cat allergies, or litter training, or who knows what the heck else. All she knew was that the beep was going off about every other minute, and none of them were to signal the information she needed. Her inbox was being flooded by tons of e-mails from people she didn't even know, and she had no idea how to stop it. "Karen, this is a very strange kind of torture," she later told me. And one we all know all too well!

How you can get someone to stop sending you pointless e-mails? It's tricky. Most people will be offended. It's just the nature of the beast. You're best off just deleting these annoying forwards. If you really need to take action, avoid telling them through e-mail, because it will always come across as rude. Pick up the phone. Monitor your voice. Speak without any hint of aggravation or stress, and you may be able to take control of the situation and make the endless e-mailing stop.

RABBIT TRICK:
FIXING AN E-MAIL MISFIRE

Problem: You've just absently hit "reply all" to an e-mail and there was someone in the chain that was not supposed to see the message you sent. What do you do?

Solution: Sadly, there is no solution to this. Depending on how egregious the e-mail, and how tolerant the mis-recipient, you could pick up the phone and try to smooth feathers—claiming a horrible day, an irrational moment, or something to that effect. This could work with a family member or friend, but if it's a client—especially a new client—the relationship is probably over.

You need to prevent it before it happens. Don't put anyone's e-mail address in the address line until you've fully composed, read, re-read, and proofread the e-mail. When you're completely certain that what's written is what you want to say, add the addressee, double check that you didn't import the wrong name from your address book, then send.

Curbing Communication

Like a Santa Ana wind, my new client, James, blew into the office, 20 minutes late, a coffee in one hand, a well-worn messenger bag in the other. He sat down at the conference room table, where I had been placed about an hour before, and where I had been patiently waiting for him to arrive.

He plunked his bag onto the table, and whipped out his cell phones, BlackBerry, and laptop, which he then flipped open. As soon as his laptop was booted up, he started to finish up revising a memo he'd started composing at home that morning.

And all of this before saying hello.

I was called in to discuss the upcoming launch of his e-business with him, but after a half an hour of watching him frantically respond to e-mail, tweak reports, and field phone calls, I had to ask him if he remembered why I was there. He looked up at me and barked, "I've had it. I have 150 e-mails just this morning. And as soon as I get around to answering them, it seems like they've already resolved themselves. I can't get anything done at this rate. I'm paying for you to be here and I can't even get to this meeting with you. I really have no idea what I should do."

I looked at him square in the face and said, "Why don't you just unplug?"

He looked at me like there were antennae sprouting out of my head. "Huh?"

"I mean, for the next hour, turn off your cell phones, hibernate your laptop, and give all your attention to me."

Are you constantly frustrated, forever behind the eight-ball, always running but never getting anywhere? Producing and producing, but still not feeling productive? There's raging mis-belief that new software developments and technological advances make us more productive. Yet, there is increasingly more research that suggests people not plugged in 24/7 are possibly more productive than those of us with electronic appendages, or who mistakenly confuse e-mail communication for life support.

E-mail can be a terrific means of communication in certain situations:

- ⊠ As a follow-up after a meeting.
- ⊠ As a way of clarifying to-do's—who has been assigned to what task.
- ⊠ As a means to hook in with others unable to attend a meeting, but who still need a real-time play-by-play of what went on.
- ⊠ As a quick way to communicate with family and friends, responding to luncheon invitations, and so forth.
- ⊠ As a way to confirm dates with the babysitter.
- ⊠ As a way to create a paper trail for someone who has trouble committing to his or her promises, and more.

E-mail has become invaluable to us in the 21st century, and it's odd to think of how we would get by in today's hectic and harried world without it. And yet, as I touched upon earlier, e-mail is also a great way to create the opposite of clarity: miscommunication and chaos.

Is Anybody Out There?!

One of the main problems people face with e-mail is getting people to respond to them. How many times have you sent an important e-mail out into the ether, only to go back to your screen 40 or 50 more times that day, clicking on the "send/receive" icon of your e-mail interface, guessing that maybe your response is stuck out there somewhere, and by sheer force of will, you can rescue it. Yes, just like the elevator comes more quickly if you keep pressing the button! Here are some useful tips to get a response too your e-mail communications:

◻ Be very specific in the subject line. Especially in our harried world of back-and-forth-and-just-hit-reply, as we use the same subject line over and over again, information can get lost forever. No one wants to be bothered excavating it. Here's an example from my own life. For the past six months I've been on a committee, but in a peripheral capacity. I receive approximately five e-mails a day from the committee chairperson. Every e-mail I have received for the past six months has the same subject line. I opened the first 50, but after being in countless chains that don't end and sifting through all the information not relevant to me, I gave up. Change your subject line as needed.

◻ Don't give your entire message in the subject line. This is a commonly employed tactic, but it can overwhelm and even backfire. Keep in mind that most people only see the first five words in the subject line, so if you have a call to action, limit it to less than five words. Make those five words count. They should be simple: "Party at Joe's Saturday night," or "CEO in town Monday only."

◻ Information and call to action aside, the subject line is a teaser, so use it that way. Take your message and drill down to the most essential thing the recipient needs to know. Instead of "I will need the books I lent you, *Who Moved My Cheese?* and *Fish* back by Monday," cut down to "Need books *Cheese?* and *Fish* back ASAP." And don't be too vague. "Playground committee," "Playground," or "Committee Meeting" are not going to tell people what they need to know. "Venue change for playground committee" gets the whole point across.

¤ Don't think of e-mail as an actual conversation. When you chat face to face with someone, you do it with a context of body language, facial expressions, and voice inflections. Even over the phone, voice comes into play. Something like sarcasm can have disastrous results in e-mail if someone's taking your joke literally.

¤ Never write in ALL CAPS, even if you think you're making a point; unless you're making it a point to annoy and alienate people. That's why you're not supposed to write in all caps, as it comes off as SCREAMING. And not to mention it's almost impossible to read. SERIOUSLY. HOW FAR WOULD YOU GET IN THIS BOOK IF THE REST OF IT WAS WRITTEN JUST LIKE THIS?

¤ Don't mistake forwarded e-mail as true involvement with a person. How special could someone think they are if they're finding out something personal about you or a special event as part of a long chain? And don't be one of those people who forwards every joke and photo and chain e-mail that comes your way. Ever hear of the boy who cried wolf? You could be known as the boy who cried crap!

¤ If you have a list of questions to which you can reply, copy and paste the question into your reply, but again, resist using ALL CAPS. Instead, why not use a bright color fonts to make your answers pop out quickly? And consider highlighting the areas that require the most urgent attention.

⌯   If you must put a lot of information in the subject line, put the most pertinent information first. "Meet you at JFK departure lounge 30 minutes before flight" is infinitely better than "For our meeting in Tulsa, we should...." Forget about stating the obvious.

⌯   Keep it short. Short e-mails (less than two quick paragraphs) will get read faster than the longer ones, which may be "saved as new" with the thought that "I'll get back to it." If you need to send a lengthy e-mail, format it as you would a Word document, in categories with headlines and subheads.

Incredible Credible

A credible person has a track record of positive results, and a proven track record of credible results. A credible person turns in competent work, well-researched, 100 percent of the time. These days, even a rate of 99.9 percent hurts your credibility.

To be credible, not only do you need to have a track record of competency, but every time you meet with someone, you have to display that. And you have to perform with sensitivity, ethics, and integrity. You're only as good as your last assignment.

So when you're trying to get through to anyone, you better make sure you at least *look* like you know what you're doing. Easier said than done? Not really.

When you deliver a message, back up what you're saying with proof. Have tangible examples to support your conclusions. Don't just flit around the issues.

When it comes to making a convincing argument remember that adjectives are cheap; you need nouns in the form of facts, statistics, persuasive data, and strong, good examples to get people to act on your message. Overusing adjectives is smoke and mirrors; eventually the smoke clears and the mirrors reveal themselves, and your credibility shatters.

Avoid hyperbole and resist the temptation to use swear words. While they may be commonplace these days, swear words are a cheap way to express emotion, and using them does not build credibility. In fact, it will diminish credibility.

Credibility is about your past, your present, and also your future. If you have aspirations about getting promoted, you have to think forward five years and start projecting and presenting that persona.

To get people on board with you, to persuade them to stand with you, you have to be able to prove to them that you are the expert. It doesn't matter if you're getting a team assembled for a special project at work or trying to get a new gardening service hired for your condominium community. You have to show that you've done your homework, that you know what you're doing, and that you're the go-to person for any questions that may arise.

But how can you show you're the expert without boasting and bragging? You have to weave in the information in tidbits of positive, successful experiences. You have to demonstrate that you're the right person, that you know what you're talking about, without reading off your resume. But how? Storytelling.

Provide historical evidence: "When I was a professor of economics at Harvard," or "When I was chair of the housing committee," or "When I was in the service," and so forth. It's all about things you say in passing, elements to flesh out the context of the story. Follow your "credential phrases" with an example such as, "What I learned was," "What we found was," "What worked in that situation," and so on.

This is not self-aggrandizing—this is providing documentation to establish credibility. You can give your track record without shooting off a laundry list of accomplishments by dropping them in an "oh, by the way" manner.

You Know You've Lost Them When...

People zone out on you. They're not going to raise their hands to tell you. Here are some signals you should be looking for:

- ¤ They're nodding in agreement with a vacant look in their eyes.
- ¤ They're not asking any questions.
- ¤ They're not asking cogent questions.
- ¤ They're not connecting the dots.
- ¤ They're not offering their opinion or additional information to advance the story.
- ¤ Their body language says "go away."
- ¤ They're chatting with the guy next to them or working on their BlackBerry.

Watch their body language: arms folded, looking down, looking through you, or nervous twitches.

Credible by Association

Can you establish credibility without correlation? Of course. Without lying, simply speak about your positive traits. Maybe you never ran a political campaign, but is there something else from your experience you could draw upon? Did you ever do any fundraising? If you have no experience, you don't have to lie. Simply make the experience you do have relevant to the topic at hand.

Listen carefully to yourself. Say you're an IT person talking about bandwidth. If you spot yourself speaking in mystery words, and you're not getting any kind of feedback, your credibility is nil. Clear it up for your listener by asking questions. Your credibility comes in the way you shape the information to fill the holes they perceive. Just be careful of the questions you ask. Don't ask: "Do you understand what I'm saying?" That can be condescending, even intimidating.

The last thing you need is for others, especially your boss, to feel diminished. If you feel like you're speaking into a black hole, don't single others out. Put the onus on yourself. Is it a bandwidth issue? Do they not understand why you need a larger one?

Bring it into their world. Use a story to which they can easily relate, and put yourself in the trenches with them: "Sometimes I have difficulty explaining this myself," you can start by saying, and then get into the moment: "Have you had problems logging on? Crashing? That's a bandwidth problem," and so forth. When you bring it into their world, using their words, and explain things without putting people down—"I'm getting ahead of myself," or "Let me get back to you"—you'll be much more credible than if you just machine-gun through your presentation, without taking your listeners into account.

TOUGH-LOVE TURNAROUND: NEW GUY COPOUT

You say: I'm new and I don't know much about the product, service, law, and opportunity as everyone else who's been working on the team.

I say: Oh, *please*. Unless you conned your way into the company (and shame on you if you did), your past experience will benefit your new team. Simply apply your experience to your new situation. It's always valuable to hear perspective from the "outside," as long as you can connect the dots to the relevancy in this situation. Your strategy in selling dentures, insurance, or cars may indeed be successful when selling stocks *if* you can connect the dots.

> The set up of the discourse is important. Don't say, "Well, when I was selling cars…" which will immediately elicit eye-rolling. Say instead, "A valuable opportunity surfaced years ago in a similar situation…what we decided to do was…. and what might work here is…" *Then* they may listen to you.
>
> Become indispensable. Become a resource. Become a problem-solver. Become proactive. Not only does nobody like a whiner, no one respects one either.

Putting on Your Game Face

The longer you're involved in your career, the more likely it will be that a situation will arise that will become insurmountable. It could be that the project you're involved in is well above your level of experience. It could be that you're having personal issues that are affecting how much focus and concentration you have for your work. It happens to everyone every now and then.

If you find yourself in this kind of situation, don't steamroll through and pretend you can handle it. Believe it or not, you'll only lose credibility that way. You can save credibility by extricating yourself from a situation—just make sure you do it with solutions to offer instead of having a meltdown in your boss's office over it. You may never be able to bounce back professionally in that environment after making a scene like that, so your best bet is to stop the snowball before it starts rolling down the hill.

I'm reminded of a woman I had hired as a consultant who was going through a very painful and messy divorce. Her estranged husband had turned her children against her; she had no one to whom she could turn, and she thought her best bet would be to throw herself into her work. Unfortunately, she was not up to the task.

She was inconsistent. She was crippled. She was completely un-credible. She wanted to prove to me that everything was okay, but the more she got into a particular project, the worse she messed it up.

She eventually sank by her own weight. Had she come to me, told me she couldn't handle the project, come clean with me, and told me she needed some time off, the situation could have resolved itself. Unfortunately, as her behavior got more erratic and clients began to complain, I had no choice but to let her go.

"There's only one thing worse than a man who doesn't have strong likes and dislikes, and that's a man who has strong likes and dislikes without the courage to voice them."
——Tony Randall

NOISE BLASTER!

Be aware of the form questions can take, and don't speculate answers if you don't have them. It's better to say, "Let me get back to you," or "I'll have to verify that with Sharon," instead of making something up that could come back to haunt you and diminish your credibility.

Consistency: Its Own Reward

You've established a good rapport with your listener. You've clearly outlined what you need for yourself, and how their contribution to the success of your endeavor will benefit them. You have dropped helpful hints along the way that show you're the right woman or man for the job. And now all your listener wants to know is this: "Can you be trusted to deliver?"

This is where consistency comes into play. People don't like surprises when they're dealing with others, they like predictability. Are you the same person every time you meet with them, or do you tend to be moody and capricious? Do you "change your spots" so often that others never know what to expect when they see you? Do people tense up when you enter a room? Nudge colleagues? Roll their eyes or turn away from you? Do they avoid meeting with you altogether—or, even worse, are they crafting a campaign to get you fired?

Presenting a consistent personality and manner is as essential to your business and personal dealings as it is to parenting. You need to be the same person delivering the same message to keep your team/group/kids where you want them; with inconsistency there's only chaos—in the conference hall/ the boardroom/the backyard.

When people don't know what they're going to get when they see you, they may just try to avoid you. Be consistent with your personality. If you're a curmudgeon, don't pretend to be sweet and nice just to get your way. If you're a lamb, a roar is going to shake people up. Be yourself. At least then we know what to expect.

Do you deliver on every project you say you're going to deliver on? Do you follow through in a timely manner? Do you give updates? When all is said and done, your reputation is all you have.

RABBIT TRICK:
I'M NOT THE ENEMY!

Problem: You've just been hired for your dream job—the one for which you've been working your entire career. You have a window, actually several of them, and a corner office larger than your first apartment. You have arrived! Except you were hired to replace a very popular person in your new firm, who was pushed out for "early retirement" and her people are still reeling from the loss. But they're yours now. You have to win them. What do you do?

Solution: You have to do whatever you can to get them on your side. What you don't want to do ever is to diminish the efforts your predecessor made as you will win no friends that way. Instead, evaluate the team and focus on their accomplishments, their ideas, and their vision. But how? Call a meet-and-greet with your direct reports and let them know they have an open forum for venting their frustrations with what happened to their former boss. Don't talk—what I mean is, don't talk a lot. Make this about them. Really listen to what they have to say, and let them know you're paying attention:

- ¤ Nod at the end of a question or comment, and pause to reflect momentarily.

- ¤ Lean forward slightly, focusing only on the person speaking. Use the person's name if possible, to demonstrate interest.

⊠ Paraphrase the person's words to re-
cap the question or challenge, and
ask if you've got it right.

⊠ Ask for more information by saying, "Tell me more about that."

⊠ Don't rush the discussion, which
could suggest that you are disinter-
ested or uncertain of your position.

⊠ Avoid emotional terms that can es-
calate a mild challenge to something
stronger.

The Bottom Line

Do they like you? Do you make them feel comfortable?
Are they getting what you're saying? Do they believe you know
what you're talking about? Are you moving forward with the
same message—or are you floundering?

There's no two ways about it: Effectively communicating
an idea to someone is a sale. A sale is a process of getting what
you want, and your end result—persuading someone to see
your side of things, arriving at an agreement, nailing the solution to a problem—is your commission.

Persuade: At a Glance

1. Have you figured out to whom you're talking and
how to conduct yourself to best appeal to that
audience?

2. Do you know exactly what you're going to say in
plain, simple English?

3. Have you worked your credentials into your message to get others to know they can trust what you're telling them?

4. Are you focused not only on talking, but listening?

5. Are you being yourself—as much as the situation allows and as much as others expect you to be?

Now that you know how to persuade an audience to your view, it's time to get up there and knock 'em dead. So in the next chapter, whether it's in a conference room, a hallway, over the phone, or during a videoconference, we'll see how to put all the strategies together to deliver an unforgettable *performance*.

STRATEGY 4

PERFORM: Putting on Your Best Show With Media Old and New

"Ever tried. Ever failed. No matter. Try again, fail
again. Fail better."
—Samuel Beckett, playwright

Performing or any kind of public speaking can be terrifying. Any kind of confrontation you need to have with another person—on a personal or professional level—can be absolutely chilling.

Why is it so scary? It all comes down to how you think you will be perceived. The flat out, hardest type of presentation to make is in front of your peers. Will your colleagues think you're credible, well-researched, and on the mark? Will they think ill of you for voicing your opinion? Are you going to fall flat on your face? Are you going to fail? Not to worry. Everyone feels this way at one time or another—even professional speakers and actors.

To perform well takes a specific kind of energy, with all your senses operating at top efficiency. Think back to the last time you went to the theater. Were there some actors who really inhabited their lines and took your breath away—and others who blended into the scenery? A great performance can turn even the most lackluster script into an Academy Award-winning show; a bad performance can destroy a literary masterpiece.

So, what do the compelling, charismatic actors *do* to create the electricity and energy that connects them with the audience? What do they know about performing that can work for the salesman, the spokesperson, the consultant—for anyone who needs to speak effectively?

Maybe you think what's important is getting the right data out there, and not your performance. I say both are equally important. To this point in the book, we've already established that your message is important, but so is taking your audience into consideration, positioning the information so that it has the greatest impact, and getting the "four Cs" of persuasion under your belt. But on top of that, *how* you deliver that information, in terms of your style, appearance, and voice inflection, is what ensures that people will remember the information (and you, too).

In this digital age, performance skills are more critical than ever. Not only do you need to be concerned with how you're coming across live and in person, but how good is your phone manner? Are you comfortable appearing in front of a camera? You better be, because videoconferences and the use of webcams are only increasing. And when you're on screen, everything becomes exaggerated and expanded, and you can quickly become less than what you are.

Scary? It can be. Unless you're skilled at presenting on camera through all media—live, teleconference, webcast, videoconference—you can seriously diminish anything else you bring to the table.

In this chapter, you will:

- Discover the five essential steps to performance perfection.
- Find out how to fend off stage fright.
- Embrace technology and see how new media can be a huge asset.

NOISE BLASTER!

How you carry yourself—your posture and body language—make up a whopping 93 percent of total image!

Step 1: Gearing Up:

Mind, Spirit, and Body

Good performing is a mental, emotional, and physical activity. So the road to performance excellence begins long before the walk to the lectern or even the boss's office on the big day. Well before you make your point, you need to get in the

"zone"—a place where your mind, spirit, and body are all aligned, a "centered" state, as actors refer to it, in which you'll have the stability, confidence, poise, and power you need to put your best foot forward on performance day. The number-one way to get in the zone is through visualization and practice, and it's part of what we'll discuss in this section.

Through the years, I've coached scores of professional athletes for product promotion appearances. Whenever possible I'll ask them how they keep their eye on the ball—literally and figuratively—and remain focused under enormous stress. Most every time, the response had to do with visualization. They visualize game day. They think about what will happen every second of the time they're on the field. They will visualize this over and over again. When game day comes, they're better able to cope with the trials and tribulations, because they've already played them out in their minds.

Well before game time, show time, or your presentation time, that's the time to start behaving like a professional athlete, a performer, and a politician even. This means taking care of your physical health, adjusting your attitude to one of optimism and love of adventure, and starting to visualize what you'll be like up there on the podium, or in front of the board room.

Read biographies of successful athletes, actors, and singers, and take tips from how they live and work. For example, many opera singers live like recluses during performance season. They don't talk on the day of the performance, and they limit the types of food they eat and the amount of alcohol and caffeine they drink. They are 100-percent focused on the task of performance.

You may not be preparing for a stage production or a game, but you need to get yourself into that mindset. Your promotion, raise, job opportunity, or political or community position absolutely depend on it.

TIPS FROM THE TRENCHES

Byron Nease
motivational speaker and star of *Phantom of the Opera*

"The most important element of presenting, no matter what the data, is to simply and directly tell the truth—whether it be in a personal story or anecdote—as sub-text or the actual speech. Audiences know when what they're hearing isn't genuine. Personalizing your information is the difference between listeners coming away with "That was okay," or "Wow! I was really moved and inspired!" The latter, the one that moves them to motivate, is always the desired effect.

"As a stage professional my entire adult life, I believe that every audience deserves an 'opening night' performance. Make no mistake—that's what you are doing. Some of it is a mindset and appropriate preparation, so you're not glued to your notes and can really make eye contact, which makes people feel like they're the only ones in the room, but part of it is physical preparation.

"When I am traveling, I arrive a day early if possible, both to acclimate and rest. That way, I can be totally focused and prepared—not frazzled and scattered from scrambling through notes quickly scribbled on the plane. It's also important to hydrate. I don't drink coffee or alcohol, and I won't consume spicy foods, or anything that may dehydrate me or give me acid reflux in mid-presentation. Your body should not be taking over your mind while you're speaking. You're there to inform and inspire your audience. It's about them, not about you."

Work It Out

If you don't do any kind of physical exercise now's the time to start. You don't want to look starched as you walk to the front of the room.

Stretch out your body. Get that body limber so you can move effortlessly and breathe efficiently throughout the day. Before you get out of bed stretch like a cat. Once you're standing upright on the floor, reach your arms up to the ceiling, inhale, hold your breath for the count of five, and slowly release it. Bend over and touch your toes; then let your arms and hands dangle in front of you.

NOISE BLASTER!

When we're stressed it seems all good eating habits go out the window. But that's the time when we need to eat smart. If nothing else, start with a healthy breakfast.

Hone the Zone

As early as one week before you have to speak, you can start getting your mind into focus and working on perfecting your performance. And you can also have a lot of fun while you're at it:

- ⌗ **Learn by example.** Head to the movies or rent some DVDs you've been meaning to see. Now, while I want you to enjoy the experience, this is not meant for entertainment only. It's more of an educational project. While you watch the stories unfold, observe other elements—the lighting, cinematography, pacing, music, choreography, and acting. Listen to the cadence of the actors' speech—not the content of the words, but the emphasis, rhythm, and timbre of their voices. Try to imitate their style. Notice that their voices get softer, louder, more excited, the more confidential in tone depending on the mood and interpretation of their part.

- ⌗ **Improve your vision.** Visit museums and study the paintings and sculpture. Imagine yourself the artist. Is there another interpretation of that scene or pose that might subtly change the meaning of the piece? Imagine a dialogue among the characters in the scene. If it is not of people, study the composition. If it's a still life, why do the fruit or flowers or what have you depicted come across the way they do? Is it the elements themselves? The texture and hues?

- ⌗ **Get moved.** Take in a concert, a ballet, or an opera. Watch how the performers move. Note the position of their hands, the expression in their eyes. Figure out how you know, just know, when they are in the moment and have become one with the audience. Study their behavior. Adapt what will work for you.

⌗ **Laugh and learn.** Head to a comedy club. Analyze what makes you laugh—is it the delivery? The physicality? Concentrate on the energy in the room. Notice how laughter makes an audience bond. Are you becoming absorbed in that energy? Watch how audience members look at each other when there is a guffaw moment, or a flash of insight into a common experience— marriage, divorce, human idiosyncrasies. In your head, try rewriting some of the skits. What would you say instead?

Visualization Exercise

Here's a quick and painless visualization exercise you can do anytime—during your commute, while you're walking through the corridors of your office, while you're driving to the super market. Whenever you have a small slice of downtime.

Imagine yourself in the moment when you are giving your presentation. Visualize…

⌗ how you look.
⌗ how you walk.
⌗ the sound of your voice.
⌗ the clarity of your words.

Hear yourself breathe—inhaling, exhaling. Feel your lungs expand and contract.

Feel the rhythm of your words as you "see" yourself opening. Feel the silence around you as you pause for emphasis.

TIPS FROM THE TRENCHES

Cabot Parsons
Parsons James Brand Architecture

"My forte is following the most off-beat idea to find a unique solution. I've done it enough times to trust my intuition, and also to realize that if it doesn't pan out, that's okay. It's not a reflection on my choice to go down that road.

"Once, for a Fortune 500 financial firm, my team was helping a research analyst put together a communication strategy for his ranking of e-commerce readiness of several corporations. Several members of the team had taken a crack at putting together this analyst's complex modeling of the elements upon which he was basing institutional investing recommendations. The stakes were high. The analyst himself had never interacted with the team; he simply sent his minions to courier our attempts and his rejections back and forth. He had a reputation for being tough and smart, but obtuse. Our various takes on creating a single PowerPoint slide to address all of the aspects of his complex model weren't clear or understandable.

"Now the ball was in my court. The first thing I did was tell his minions to bring him down to our conference room, where my team and I had all gathered together. I then asked him to explain the model to me. I listened for quite some time. While technical, the pieces and parts of the model were all easily understandable, and the analyst was both thorough and compelling. When he finished, I took a moment, and came up with the solution. I said: 'What we need to do is just send you out personally with the model and have you explain it to everybody!'

"After the laughter died down, I began to explore an idea that did exactly that. Instead of a deck presentation or binder or incomprehensible slide, we created a door-size poster that was a large, multi-paneled comic strip, starring a cartoon version of our analyst. He had a great reputation in his industry, but was known for being quite dry. For that reason, our idea to present him as a combination between "Mr. Science" and a used-car salesman was a true departure—much to the delight of his audience.

Throughout the course of several panels, we had him explain the e-commerce chain, with fun asides from several other characters, as he introduced his model. We even had the cutout of him riding part of his model like a bucking bronco.

At the end of reading this poster, a horse race-type graphic showing his investment pics relative to his model was understandable and compelling. And the institutional investors who received this poster not only got valuable information, but also a great conversation piece.

> The analyst became a bit of a celebrity
> with his peers, because he'd had the nerve
> to make his points at his own expense and
> communicate in a manner that was clearest,
> rather than taking the road most traveled.

Creativity Out of Bounds

Do you ever feel like there's a box around you, forcing you to conform to a preconceived notion of what a presentation should be like? Well, it's time to break free of those constraints and really let your creativity flow.

Start thinking outside the box. Try pushing ordinary situations to absurd conclusions; this is where comedians excel. A late-night talk show host once included a recent health crisis at a fast-food restaurant in his monologue. The crisis was a disaster for this restaurant. A video of rats walking on tables and on counter tops, eating crumbs left over from diners, was all over the Internet. The comic looked at the situation through the rats' eyes, noting how fat and happy the rats looked, and how shiny their coats were. "The food must be nutritious," he quipped. The point here is that when you examine issues from all perspectives you can not only alleviate tension, but can also unlock inspired phrasing and juxtaposition of ideas for your presentation.

Years ago, I was working with a jingle writer from Nashville, helping him sell his jingles to advertising agencies in New York. I thought it was fascinating to observe that specific kind of talent. We'd go into agencies and the creative directors would play the jingles. Often, they'd ask my client to rework one on the spot.

I wanted to know how he pulled off that instant creativity, because I felt it could help business people think out of the box when creating presentations. When I asked him how, he told me he takes a topic and turns it upside down. Similar to the comedian with the rat, he took the opposite point of view. So, for example, if talking about love, turn it on its ear by listing all the reasons you don't hate the person or thing. Use this technique and you may just discover comedic, insightful, and perhaps even profound ways of looking at situations—even in business. At the very least, it's an enjoyable exercise to get your creative juices flowing and to loosen up your presentation so that it is more conversational and engaging.

This is a skill at which my friend, political satirist Rock Albers, excels. He'll take a current event and push it to an absurd, unrealistic end point. What remains is a hilarious yet provocative, and sometimes frightening, scenario. So what's especially brilliant about his approach?

At one of his shows, Rock was talking about a discussion currently in the United States about non-natural-born Americans being allowed to run for president through a constitutional amendment. He took it further. Why should we stop there? Why not try and elect a president who's not even living in the US? Tony Blair needs a job. Yes, this is unrealistic, but all the while that you're laughing you're thinking and wondering, gee, what if….

RABBIT TRICK:
RALLYING THE TROOPS

Thanks to Patricia Diaz Dennis, chair of the National Board of Directors for Girl Scouts of the USA, senior vice president and assistant general counsel for AT&T Inc., for her insight on this Rabbit Trick.

Problem: You're in the position of having to filter the needs and wants of an eclectic group made up of very different people, from all levels—who have very different issues, ideas, opinions, and attitudes—that all need to be addressed. How do you handle it?

Solution: "I speak plainly, directly, and honestly to everyone, from the worker at the bottom of the totem pole all the way on up. I use real language because far too many people speak in acronyms and terms of art that others don't get right away.

"I acknowledge the difficult issues or the weak spots. The acknowledgement gains trust.

"I also appeal to people's hearts, because, if you can get to their hearts, their minds will follow. Providing the proper context is an important tool I use. At Girl Scouts of the USA, I start each board meeting by having girl representatives come in and speak to us about their experiences and why they're Girl Scouts. This approach has really worked as a reality check for us board members. When we listen to the girls talk about

> how Girl Scouting has affected their lives, as well as how we can do better, the Board is able to stop and refocus on our true purpose. Everything we do needs to benefit girls. The visual creates a visceral reaction and causes people to take our mission to heart. A byproduct is an opportunity for these wonderful young women to gain confidence in speaking before an audience.
>
> "I've found illustrating my point with metaphors and telling personal stories are other fantastic ways to help people grasp messages quickly and entirely. The moral points of fables make an impression because they're in story form."

Take Them at Hello

There are many exciting ways to capture an audience at the get-go. Though, unfortunately, in my experience the most-often-used opening statement sounds something like this: "Good morning. It's a pleasure to be here today," which is followed by a laundry list of housekeeping details and ground rules for the presentation (please turn off cell phones, restrooms are located here and there, there will be two breaks lasting 10 minutes each, and so forth).

And I can *guarantee* you that, in this 500-channel, multitasking, barely-listening universe in which we live, if you start your meeting with nothing substantive you will deplete the room of anticipatory energy.

Let's revisit the show business analogy. Say you bought a ticket to a show a year ago and the day of the performance has finally arrived. You're excited. You're dressed up. You're sitting sixth row center orchestra.

And then there's an announcement: The headliners you've come to see are all sick. Then the third-tier understudy walks onto the stage and begins reading from the script. How do you feel?

Well, that's how your audience will feel if you walk on and say nothing substantive in the first few minutes.

Yes, giving housekeeping details is important (and, in some sectors mandatory), but you can show them on a slide or put them in the agenda. Tell the audience a little later, but not during your opening salvo. The intro has got to hit them; if you appeal to their interests, their needs, and their desires in the first 30 seconds, you will capture them.

TIPS FROM THE TRENCHES

Mary Jo Roberts
Independent Mannatech Health Consultant

"I have spent most of my life being terrified of speaking in public. I have given up many career advancements because I would not and could not speak in front of even a small group of people.

"Six years ago, I decided to start learning how to overcome this fear. First, I was coached by a team at CommCore Strategies in New York City.

"Next step, I joined Business Network International. I give a 60-second presentation every week in front of 30 to 40 people. I always write down my speech in advance of the presentation. I practice in front of a mirror, over and over.

Before the meeting, I visualize giving the speech. When it is time to speak, I take several deep breaths, walk to the front of the room, and smile. When all eyes are on me, instead of being frightened, I think that these people are very eager to hear what I have to say. I am still nervous, but I can do it and have been told I do it well."

Great Grabbers

Here are some suggested openers that will really get—and keep—their attention:

- ⌑ **The Hook.** "I've been traveling around the world this year and I'm here to tell you why working and living in Asia can help propel your career forward."

- ⌑ **The Tease.** "During this presentation, I will be giving you next year's incentive plan. But let's start with the state of the company."

- ⌑ **The Quiz.** "There are five reasons why we will win this contest. Can anyone tell me what they think these are?"

- ⌑ **The Shock.** "The competition is outdoing us by 35 percent, but I can tell you how to get our numbers up."

Once you've appealed to their needs, don't fall into the trap of delivering only facts. Remember when you've been in the position of having to endure a speaker drone on about research or give a long, detailed history about a topic without giving any context of *why* it's relevant. You know this kind of thing has left you squirming in your seat, your eyes rolling, or your brain miles away. If you have to barrage listeners with facts, at least tease them a bit. Drop little nuggets of incentive, for they can enjoy it if they're paying attention. Keep stimulating them with signal phrases (see the strategy on *persuading*) like "A little known fact is," " What I've learned is," "The inside scoop is." By giving them something that makes them feel like they've just penetrated the inner circle, they'll feel special and bonded to you for the duration.

NOISE BLASTER!

A person may momentarily zone out during your presentation—it's not necessarily you. Just don't look at that person nodding off. Look at the people who are giving you positive feedback and interact with them.

Stage Fright

There is no fear like performance fear. It has nearly crippled great singers and actors who you'd never think would have stage fright. Barbra Streisand spent years avoiding concert tours after she forgot the lyrics to a song during her 1968 Central Park concert. Only after she got help from a doctor and a started taking a beta-blocker used to treat high blood pressure did she resume touring. Carly Simon was also concert-phobic, and reportedly has been known to pass out from the stress of live performing.

Even though I have spent decades assisting speakers in their quest for calmness during their speeches, it still amazes me when a polished, exemplary speaker asks: "What do I do about the knot in my stomach any time I walk on stage?" Even I suffer from stage fright. So many of the tips I'll give you in this section are those that have actually helped me.

Hang on. I'm trying to find something more interesting than you.

Think Back

The first thing I recommend to people when they are worried about an upcoming meeting or presentation is to try and
recall a successful business situation in which they felt validated and performed well—speaking up in a meeting, having a
productive discussion with the boss, or successfully managing
an issue with a difficult team member.

I ask them: Were you nervous beforehand? Probably. And
then I tell them that no matter how nervous they had felt at
the time, there was still a successful conclusion. There isn't
anything quite as grounding as remembering positive outcomes
and then translating the attitude and composure to your present
situation.

Look Ahead

We've already addressed it in this chapter, but visualization is also a very powerful antidote to overwhelming nerves.

Homeopathic and Rx Therapies

Many people have found temporary relief from performance jitters by using homeopathic products such as
Gelsemium or Agrimony, orby taking a very small dose of a
beta-blocker. These treatments are merely Band-Aids, and not
long-term help with behavior modification, but if you wish to
explore these options, please do so only under a physician's
guidance. I typically don't recommend using them.

Move Your Body

Many performers who have excelled despite crippling stage
fright have found their center of calmness through Yoga.

Additionally, daily walks, a short jog, walking on the elliptical, or any type of aerobic exercise will energize you and calm your nerves, so on the days leading up to your presentation, build a 30-minute regimen into your daily schedule.

Think Nutrition

I'm not here to be your mother, but at least on performance day, have a light breakfast with lots of protein, such as multigrain bread, or cereal, and limit your caffeine.

Breathe

The single best antidote to stage fright is deep breathing prior to walking on stage and then taking deep belly breathes between sequences during your presentation. The more shallow the breath the more off balance you can become.

The Evan Situation

Evan, a well-known medical clinician and researcher turned heads anywhere he went, as his tall, lanky frame strolled down hospital corridors greeting colleagues and patients. The doctor and researcher had a beautiful speaking voice, and was a recognized thought leader in his medical specialty. But he had demons, which would surface only when he was called upon to speak to his peers on stage at scientific symposia.

What haunted the man, I'll never know, but when I learned about the case I was given only two days to help him before he had to speak in front of a thousand people, as well as be interviewed by the national news media.

It was a major news event for his medical field. Because he was the lead investigator, he had been chosen to announce the results of a clinical study. But the sponsoring organization was worried because of his public speaking history.

In his workaday world, Evan was king of the jungle. He was always in control and used to giving the orders. But outside the research facility and hospital he felt out of control and pathologically vulnerable. In fact, it was not unusual for him to suddenly disappear when he had to present, having to take an emergency call or some such excuse. Someone else always had to jump in and present in his place. Later, in a roundtable discussion, away from the spotlight, he was able to discuss his findings.

The excuses were wearing thin, so I was called in to coach him.

On the first day, I met with Evan in a small conference room at the convention center. I always work with video and playback, but it didn't seem like the best approach in this situation. I also had a small audio tape recorder.

I was mystified to find, in the center of the table, a pitcher of martinis. The consulting firm that had hired me thought it would be a good way to loosen him up. I ordered some tea, coffee, and warm water with lemon as well as a plate of cookies, and quietly told the caterers to remove the alcohol.

As tempting as it is to drink liquor before a performance, I can guarantee it's not going to elevate your credibility. Think back to all the concert singers you've seen who were drunk at the microphone. Not a pretty picture.

As Evan and I started chatting, he was becoming increasingly anxious, so I suggested we take a walk. As we strolled through the gardens, I asked him when he felt most relaxed. As we got to know each other and he went more and more into the world he loves—boating—I encouraged him to visualize the feeling he gets from the air, smell of the bay, the sun in his face. We went over that scenario about 20 or 30 times.

When he seemed relaxed, I suggested we go back inside and look at the presentation he needed to make. I told him that if we could inject some boating analogies into his narrative or at least tell a story about boating, it could help lead to a point he needed to make in the presentation. "If you can mention something about boating a few times during your 40-minute talk," I explained, "you can use these as triggers to relax you."

We spent the next several hours dissecting the presentation and finding places where references to boating could be made.

When we met on the second day, he was again nervous, so I asked him to spend 10 minutes talking about boating. Then I took out my audio player and told him to tell me again and I would tape it.

Gradually, we moved to videotaping and feedback; to more rehearsing, and more visualization.

Later that afternoon, Evan walked out on stage. He stood quietly for two seconds, looked out over the room, and gave his introduction, which included a reference to boating.

I can't say that Evan loves public speaking even now, but because he was able to bring into it a calming influence, he can at least manage it.

Step 2: Breathe

Shallow breathing and vocal chord strain are among the biggest contributors to fatigue in the work place. We don't realize how much energy we use when we talk. As I have my professional roots in both broadcasting and vocal performance, I have seen a lot of abuse done to voices by busy executives.

My vocal coach, Phil Hall, told me a story about himself that might be useful to you. He said, "Years ago, I used to speak in run on sentences. This isn't a good habit for a singer. I had nearly fried my vocal cords by never stopping to take a breath." When I asked him what he did about it, he replied that he had seen an ear, nose, and throat doctor, who recommended

TIPS FROM THE TRENCHES

Phil Hall
New York City-based vocal coach

"For stage fright and to calm the nerves at auditions, I recommend students do a deep breathing exercise they've tried at home, so they're familiar with it when they need it most. It's a yogic-based breathing exercise. To demonstrate it, I lie down on the floor, and take a large book like an oversized dictionary (one can strap several books together with a fastener or belt) and place it on my abdomen. I take a deep breath—distending the abdomen in a yogic fashion, and, as I prepare to slowly hiss the sound out, I use both hands and pull down very strongly on the book, causing my abdominal muscles to resist caving in to the pressure my hands and the book are applying as I continue to slowly hiss out the breath.

"When I'm done, I relax for a minute or two, and then I repeat this sequence approximately four times. After the fourth time, again, I rest for about two minutes before slowly getting up to a seated position, and then getting up all the way. (I do this before getting up in case I've gotten light-headed doing the exercise.) At an audition, I encourage students to do the same sequence seated in an upright position, and, of course, without the book."

that he slow down his speech and force himself to breathe between phrases. "For one full week, I paused a few seconds between each thought and breathed," he told me. "I know I drove everyone around me nuts, but it was the only way I was able to break the habit. Not only was I able to save my vocal cords, as an added bonus, I learned to organize my thoughts more succinctly since the breaths allowed me additional time to decide what I was going to say."

Exercise for Breath and Voice Control

1. Put your fists on your chest and push them down, saying: Ha, hay, he, hay, ho, ho, ma, may, me, my, mo, moo; na, nay, ne, ny, no, noo; repeat again. *This exercise will help you project sound better.*

2. Inhale as much air as you can; exhale very slowly and steadily. Learn to lengthen your exhalation period to 25 seconds and more. Repeat three times a day. *This exercise will build diaphragm muscles and increase vocal endurance.*

3. Shake or rock your jaw from right to left and back again as fast as possible. While rocking your jaw, produce a tone (around G or A for women, for men around G1 or A1). Move up and down the music scale first with and then without jaw rocking. *This exercise will increase your ability to phrase better and create a mood.*

4. Yawn on a sound, such as "ouya," while simultaneously exhaling. Chew the sound while yawning. Hum on "m" as long as you can. Chew words containing "m" and "n" sounds, such as "come home, my mum, name," and so on. *This exercise will help enunciation.*

Vocal Dis-chord?

You want to avoid this at all costs, so make sure you take care of your voice. Most of us are on conference calls much of the day—often conducted over speaker phone—or we're yelling on cell phones in order to be heard. Speaker phones and cell phones are major culprits in creating vocal distress, but we can't stop using them altogether. So how can you use these tools and not abuse your voice? The next time you're on a speaker phone, listen to how your voice tenses up when you're raising it in order to be heard. Do you feel your neck muscles squeezing together? Pay attention to how tight your larynx feels. That can be devastating to your voice in the long term.

Think about politicians and how many times you've heard them screech through an attack of laryngitis. Not only is it uncomfortable for them to speak, it's uncomfortable for us to hear. And what's worse, it can be a credibility buster. If the person can't take care of his or her voice, how can he or she take care of the country? Or the company? Or even run the Ladies Auxiliary's next bachelor auction?

Vocal Gymnastics

There's a joke about people putting the em-PHA-sis on the wrong syl-LA-ble, but it's actually a huge consideration when you want to create impact. Consider this sentence:

You can bet on it happening.

You can change the meaning of this phrase depending on your vocal tone and inflection:

YOU can bet on it happening.
Okay, so this is for *you*!

You CAN bet on it happening.

Okay, so I can trust you're going to take care of this for me.

You can BET on it happening.

Okay, so I can be so sure it *will* happen, I can put money on it.

You can bet on IT happening.

So the "it" is so important that thank goodness it will finally happen!

You can bet on it HAPPENING.

We've been in a stall pattern so long, so hooray that we'll finally have movement here!

One phrase, five ways. Each has a different meaning and delivers a different meaning. The lesson to be learned here? Pay attention to where the emphasis falls as emphasizing the correct word can be motivational; emphasizing the wrong word can be confusing and, worse, demoralizing.

Step 3: Practice

You have your words planned. You've pictured yourself saying them in front of your audience again and again. Now, you need to see how you come across. I use videotaping in my workshops to help people experience exactly how they come across. There is no better tool. Short of that approach, I suggest standing in front of a mirror. Keep in mind though that a mirror is exactly that—a mirror image. I'm sure you know that the right side of the body is a bit different than the left side. It's a much better representation of the real you with the videotape practice. And videotaping is an exact image.

You can more easily give yourself to your audience—real or imagined—by videotaping your practice sessions. When

5-MINUTE PLAN OF ATTACK

Once you've created the video, it's time to review it, but wait 10 minutes. Grab a cup of coffee and sit back to enjoy the show. Now watch the video as though you would a movie—as if it isn't really you up there. Wait another 10 minutes to give yourself time to digest what you saw, then start the following five steps:

Minute 1: Write down what was appealing about the person on the screen (and be fair to yourself).

Minute 2: Write down what came across in attitude. Did you like the person on the tape?

Minute 3: Write down how your voice sounded, along with your inflection, phrasing, tone, clarity, and emphasis.

Minute 4: What about your body language—gestures, eye contact, posture, facial expression? Write down your thoughts.

Minute 5: Write down the takeaway point (please don't refer back to your notes—do it from memory).

My goal is to build your confidence, which is why I urge you to try videotaping. If you choose this approach you can maximize your efforts and make the process as painless as possible.

standing in front of a mirror you can't escape yourself, and the practice sometimes ends up less productive and more sterile then it would be in real life.

Nobody—not celebrities, movie stars, or politicians—enjoys watching themselves on tape, but all agree it's the best learning device there is. When I'm coaching people I'll first put them on camera for a short segment—2 to 5 minutes long. I suggest you do that also. The goal of this exercise is for you to demonstrate that you can communicate the bottom line.

Visual Tips

1. Do your presentation first, then do your slides and visual aids. The visuals are there to support and help explain your topic.

2. Simplify, simplify! Keep the slide as simple as possible. If you do have to use a complex slide use yellow highlighting to make the key points stand out.

3. Make it visual. Add pictures, videos, and photos to enhance the slide. Graphic elements must relate to your topic.

4. Use color. Audience retention increases exponentially when color is used. Use red and green cautiously, however, because many people have red/green color blindness. High-contrast combinations such as blue backgrounds with white and yellow lettering work well.

5. Use PowerPoint shortcuts:
   ¤ B key turns screen black (toggle).
   ¤ W key turns screen white (toggle).
   ¤ Home key jumps to first slide.
   ¤ End key jumps to end.
   ¤ Any number key jumps to that slide.

⌑   H key hides pointer.

⌑   F1 key during a show brings up shortcut key list.

Digital Dancing

The biggest bugaboo about using visuals—aside from the fact that there is generally far too much information on a slide—is the lack of transitions *between* the slides. How many times have you heard presenters say: "On this slide," or "This slide says," and then proceed to read every word on the slide? To be effective, every slide needs to have an intro and an exit line, and there needs to be a transition—a 10-word phrase that sets up the slide.

Step 4: Dress the Part

"Dress the part" is about what you wear on your back, but your appearance means much more than your clothes. It's your hair and your makeup, your shoes and accessories. The way you carry yourself in the skin you are in. We've touched on customizing your style and feeling comfortable presenting your message as "yourself." This next section is really just about how you should actually look.

Clothing

Business dress has become more relaxed in the past decade, though in some sectors, there has been a return from business casual to more formal attire. When the custodial and security staff is better dressed and groomed than the executives, one starts to wonder whose setting the more professional tone in the company.

The more global we become in our business dealings the more we will integrate the habits of our international

5-MINUTE PLAN OF ATTACK

During a practice session, print out your slides and lay them out in the order in which you've designed them. Now:

Minute 1: Review the color choices of the slides. What is your background color? Blue is best with black text with yellow or white for headings.

Minute 2: Review the font and print pitch. Can you walk across the room and still see what is written? Your audience needs to *easily* read your slides. They'll tune you out if they can't.

Minute 3: Walk around the table. Take in the story. Think carefully: Does what you're saying here really need a slide? Do you really need so much information on the slide? Could it be a bar chart, graph, or other illustration rather than lines of text?

Minute 4: With a tape recorder in hand, press the record button, go from slide to slide, and quickly say the intro and exit line. If you can quickly think and say the transition then the slide is in the correct position. If you struggle, rethink the order of slides.

Minute 5: Walk around the table and say the key take-away message out loud. You only have a minute, so you can speak in bullet points. If you can tell yourself the key, take-it-to-the-bank message under this kind of pressure, then you've got it nailed.

colleagues. I travel internationally extensively, and I'm always impressed by the image that people from developing nations project with their decorum. It's a pleasant throwback to a more elegant time in business etiquette and dress. There is a cottage industry springing up where etiquette coaches are teaching manners and dress to young executives, who are rolling out of universities still donning the jammies that they wore to class.

My philosophy is that every 10 years we all should all get an image makeover. We express different attitudes and looks depending on the seasons of our career. When you're a junior account executive at an ad agency you may wish to present an edgier look than when you're the CEO of a multinational corporation. While I don't believe people should be a slave to fashion it's critical to stay on top of trends and adapt them for yourself, if for no other reason than to blend in—and I mean that in the best way.

For example, I know a mid-level executive who is very ambitious, but can't make the cut for a promotion to a director slot. She is unkempt; her long hair hangs in her eyes. She wears no makeup, sloppy khakis, T-shirts, and sneakers. If you look at her boss who is very well groomed and dresses casually, but well, she has obviously put time into getting trained in appropriate business demeanor. She may not be as smart or as clever as her underling, but I bet she'll get the promotions. Is it fair? Nope. But that's the way it is, so its better to deal with it now.

If you're in an industry that embraces casual work attire, my recommendation for presentation day would be for you to dress at least one notch better than you would ordinarily. You're there to project confidence and competence. A sloppy T-shirt and jeans or a halter top with your belly ring exposed might not quite garner the positive attention you're seeking. You're trying to move up the ladder, not down.

NOISE BLASTER!

Depending on your industry, be appropriate in terms of flamboyant or conservative. What's appropriate? Err on the side of conservatism.

Men: Business Casual

⊠ Khakis.

⊠ Button-down shirt with a collar and preferably long sleeves. Blue is always a good choice for a shirt, but prints are acceptable as well.

⊠ Even for "casual," a tie is a nice touch.

⊠ A sport jacket would be an enhancement, but if your company is very informal, you may feel uncomfortable and over-dressed for an office meeting.

⊠ Shoes should be loafers or oxfords with a leather sole. Please, no sneakers on presentation day.

⊠ While it may seem obvious, socks are an important contribution to proper business attire.

Men: Business Formal

⊠ Business suit. For presentations, pinstriped is popular and will stand the test of time, so, do invest in at least one good suit.

⊠ White or colored shirts.

⊠ Interesting but not overly busy patterned ties. Tastefully and subtly mixing prints and plaids can work in your favor. The keyword here is *tastefully*.

If you have doubts take a trusted friend with you to a proper men's clothing store.

NOISE BLASTER!

When you're getting in front of a group to speak, turn off your BlackBerry and/or cell phone—and remove them from your belt.

Women: Business Casual

⌕ Slacks.

⌕ Full length or three-quarter length sleeved sweater or blouse either tucked in or worn on the outside of the slacks. A two-inch decorative belt would be a nice touch if the blouse is worn outside the slacks. If the sweater has a low décolletage, you might consider wearing a cami underneath it for the business meeting. Low necklines are pretty, except when they look more like cocktail lounge clothing rather than conference room.

⌕ Jewelry nowadays is more on the embellished side than a few years ago. Chandelier earrings are very trendy, however, I would avoid them for presentations. Why? The earrings waving in the breeze as you enthusiastically present your budget numbers can be distracting. Dangly earrings could be an attractive choice as long as they don't extend down to the chin line. Wear earrings no longer than an inch below your earlobe.

⌂   Necklaces can be a very attractive enhancement as long as they don't take over the outfit. Bracelets can be fun as long as they don't sound like a drum beat as your arm hits the table during your talk.

Women: Business Formal

⌂   Suits are always appropriate. The jacket and skirt don't have to be matched as long as the fabric design and texture are compatible with each other.

⌂   Wear some color, either as the jacket, or the blouse or camisole, underneath the jacket. (Blouses worn on the outside of the skirt and a little longer than the jacket make an otherwise formal look become business-presentation casual.)

⌂   Shoes should be comfortable enough that you're not shifting your weight from one foot to the other—you like stilettos, great. If you can afford shoes from Jimmy Choo, Feragamo, or other very high-end shoe designers that are built for beauty, comfort, and stability, go for it. But if you're like the vast majority of us who can't afford $800 shoes, go for the two-inch pumps that will give you a finished look, but still allow you to keep your balance. Please, no flip flops on presentation day.

Makeup

There's something refreshing about the unmade-up face *if* you're 20 years old and have unblemished skin, beautiful long-lashes, and perfect teeth. Otherwise, if you want to project a polished, professional, ambitious, "got it together" attitude and look, consider getting a makeup consultation from a qualified makeup and image expert. Minimal effort and minimal makeup—a bronzer, blush, light lipstick, and eyeliner can turn frump into fabulous in five minutes.

Step 5: Grab 'Em and Never Let Go

The big day has finally arrived. Your slides are finalized and your content has been approved. You've practiced your presentation, and you're in a great new, comfortable outfit. You had a decent breakfast. You had a good night's sleep, and you're rested and focused.

Before you head out to the stage, podium, or conference room, take a few minutes to limber up. Stretch, relax, and do your breathing exercises. Take a brisk 30-minute walk—either outside or on the treadmill. While you're working out, work through your agenda. Ask yourself over and over again:

- ⌑ What's the purpose of this presentation?
- ⌑ What do I want from it?

Know the answers cold. Now visualize where you're going to speak—an auditorium? A small cluttered conference room? Get your head in the moment.

And Now Introducing...

The moment is here. You're all assembled in whatever venue you happen to be meeting in and your turn is now.

Be quietly enthusiastic. Wait until you're introduced to stand and walk to the front of the room. Don't start talking while you're walking up to the front of the room. Keep your mic turned off while you're seated. You have no idea what inappropriate, hurtful, stupid comments have blared over the P.A. system because a presenter forgot to turn off his microphone.

Once you reach your destination, don't start talking right away. Get your breath. Now, go for your grabber.

As you speak, use natural gestures. By these, I mean the ones that come from the shoulder, not the elbow. Loose shoulders are natural. Tense shoulders make your gestures unnatural. Your arms will look like lobster claws. No one will be listening to you. They'll be watching your freakish arms, and that's not what you want. Before you head to the front of the room, shake your arms and shoulders out, and keep them loose as you speak.

Work to connect with your audience. Look to a section of the room. Make eye contact with a person and hold it for a complete thought. Keep doing this with different areas of the room and your tone will naturally become conversational—like you're chatting with one person and one person alone; at least for that minute or so.

Presentation Perfection

I've dedicated the better part of my life to coaching presenters to make sure they get what they want from the presentation. Otherwise, what's the point? If your presentation is flawlessly written yet your performance lands flat, it's better to stay home and e-mail your presentation to the audience.

As mentioned earlier, presentations written for the ear utilize a shorter sentence structure than sentences written for the eye. In written communication, you have the benefit of commas, semi-colons, and colons that we can't hear when you're speaking. So, shorten your sentences.

To key into aural communication, listen to rhythm of the spoken word from professional speakers, like news anchors. Watch how they breathe, taking deep belly breaths from the diaphragm rather than a shallow hiccup of a breath from the throat. Listen to how they modulate their voices, change the pacing of their speech. They vary their patterns to keep us tuned in.

TOUGH-LOVE TURN-AROUND: THE WALLFLOWER

You say: I have lots to say, but no one ever asks for my opinion.

I say: Oh come on. It's your responsibility to offer your thoughts. I have a friend who always feels excluded because no one solicits her thinking. Well, it never occurred to her that people *may not know* she has opinions. You have to speak up. Most of us are too busy to go out of our way to ask for input. We'll gravitate to the person who satisfies our needs the fastest.

If you don't want to get lost in the sauce, speak up. Don't wait for someone to call on you. This isn't the fourth grade. If you want your opinions known, you have to voice them. End of story.

If people would spend even 50 percent of the time working on their performance skills that they spend on editing and reediting their slides, I believe we wouldn't all dread going to meetings as we do. Nowadays, the rules for the "perfect presentation" have loosened up just as rules for dress have become more relaxed in the work environment. Add to that the more casual approach to delivering news on TV, and the growth and artificial coziness the Internet offers us; we are able to appear more human and less robotic than the "official" presentation style of even a few years ago.

When I coach people, I first observe their personalities. Then, as we work together, I shape the skills to their specific needs instead of taking a one-size-fits-all approach. In all my years of doing this, I've learned that people aren't going to fundamentally change their personality. You are who you are. But you can modify certain physical gestures or facial expressions, so you don't distract from your message.

Find what works for you and what doesn't. For example, some people need to move about when presenting. Fine. Move. But, here's the caveat: If you continue to pace back and forth across the room, a rhythm will develop, and suddenly the audience, without even realizing it, will be focused on your pacing as opposed to listening to you. Their heart rate will accelerate because your constant moving is making them anxious. So if you like to move, move to one side of the room and angle your body so that your face is turned three-quarters toward the other side. The people on your angled side get your "presence," and the people on the other side get more eye contact. Then, after a few paragraphs or to the count of 20, move again. With so many meetings configured in a U-shape, this is an ideal way to keep people's attention. And be sure to use a body microphone as opposed to a lectern mic, which of course allows for movement.

Get Equipped

Amplification is critical for big room presentations. Even if the audience is only 15 or 20 people, you might want to request a mic. Amplification helps you save your voice as well as manage distractions, interruptions, and oddball occurrences. This is especially important if it's an offsite meeting at a hotel or conference center, and the ambient noise in the room is significant, or where there very likely will be meetings in the next room (separated from yours only by a thin accordion screen).

I remember giving a speech at such a place and next door was a calypso band playing a wedding reception. My presentation was punctuated by the high siren sound of trumpets. Talk about distractions. I ended up playing with that distraction and pretending the trumpets were my accompaniment. I changed the rhythm of my speaking to match the rhythm of the band. After the initial shock of the distraction wore off and I adjusted, it ended up being hugely fun.

Argue for amplification. A body mic is best, because it will free you up and allow you to move about. However, if you're stuck at a lectern microphone, be careful not to turn away and look at the screen to point out details, for we will lose your voice during those moments.

A few years ago, I was in a meeting where an official from a regulatory agency was speaking. The subject was of some seriousness having to do with marketing of pharmaceuticals. He was at the lectern, and had the unfortunate habit of stating very important information with his back turned to audience, reading his slides off the screen instead reading off the monitor sitting directly in front of him. Nobody could hear him.

NOISE BLASTER!

Be sure that speaking in front of a crowd is not the first time you've spoken all day. If you have no opportunity to have a conversation with someone, at least speak your lines until you get to where you'll be presenting that day.

I'll never forget the frustration mixed with muted humor from the audience, because he would signal that something important was coming by saying, "Now this is critical," and proceed to turn away from us, waving his laser pointer at the screen.

Your 15 Minutes Have Arrived!

The local morning talk show has just invited you to talk about your company's new product, but you've never appeared on TV before. So what should you do?

First, watch the program—even if you're already familiar with it. Get to know the style of the interviewer. Get into the spirit of the show. If they use sarcasm and like to spar, learn to go with the flow. TIVO it, tape it. By all means study it.

On the day of the interview, come a half an hour earlier than you're supposed to. If you can walk around the set before it begins, do it. (Try not to trip over the cables.) Get comfortable. There are dozens of engineers, technicians, and directors wandering around, and this can make you anxious.

Take your seat on the set. Have a look around and breathe. Focus on keeping yourself grounded. When the host slides in the chair next to you, you'll suddenly hear "3-2-1," and then the host will start talking. Look at the host, not at the camera, and put yourself in a mode of polite conversation. If you're tall, lean back in the chair. If you're short, do not cross your legs. It will throw you into the back of the chair and clinch your diaphragm.

The TV is a small box. It's a small screen. You don't see the bigness of a Broadway stage. Use your face and eyes to express emotion. Use natural gestures to relieve anxiety—alleviate tension, and animate your voice and your face. Before you go on, relax your neck and shoulders.

An interview goes by like a speeding train. If you stiffen, the audience will notice. You want to convey an interesting relaxed demeanor, and keep your focus on getting your message across. We'll talk more about steering messages back when someone tries to take you off course in the next chapter.

NOISE BLASTER!

In this overly digitalized world, there is a natural temptation to overdo graphics by using the technology too often, in the wrong formats, and with too much elaboration. The result can create a noise of its own, overwhelming or trivializing the core message.

Bogs of Blogs

In *Internet for Dummies*, the authors define the process of blogging, or creating a web-log, and follow up the glossary entry to blogging with this phrase: "Any fool can publish a blog, and many fools do." What it comes down to is that any information on the Internet is suspect unless you know for a fact that you are reading a credible and validated source. If you are thinking of managing a blog, you need to be *that* credible source.

If you're an entrepreneur, it's imperative that you have a blog. It's a terrific way to grow your business beyond a Website. In fact, many people are now opting to develop a Blog instead of a Website.

TIPS FROM THE TRENCHES

Steve Kyler
director of IT Solutions, AVI Inc.

"It has been my experience that more and more clients want to Webcast, but still don't understand the true power of content and meetings delivered via the Internet, and eventually opt for more traditional solutions. Typically, after a successful Web event, we hear from the client again and again and they continue to try and widen the scope and scale of their next event. Despite Webcasting being around for quite a while, similar to most meeting technology, it's been slow to adopt. The prevalence of faster bandwidth and lower-costing, high-quality equipment is closing the gap pretty fast. The number of inquiries we received in 2007 was almost 300 percent greater than the requests in 2006.

"Webcasts are actually very easy to produce, if you have the right equipment. You're taking live content into a box and squeezing it down. As for content selection, you have to envision the output—you're not going to see a 9×12 screen. Graphics cannot be small, colors cannot be white on white—we will not see these clearly on a Webcast. You need to light the environment for television. And just like television, a good Webcast has a beginning, a middle, and an end; consider how each of those is supposed to look, and feel.

"Bandwidth matters. Not just the bandwidth on the event side, but also on the receiving side. Webcasts are typically pushed to a group of servers, then retrieved by the viewer; this creates 'latency,' which is a delay anywhere from 30 seconds to five minutes.

"Lastly, not all encoding devices are the same—this is truly a medium in which you get what you pay for. Here is a good rule of thumb: If it looks like a toaster—it makes toast, if it looks like it powers a Website, it is probably a Webcasting server. Ask for samples, ask about bandwidth, ask about 'load balanced servers.' If the guy on the other end of the discussion can't answer those things intelligently, you're going to have trouble."

Perform: At a Glance

1. Have you gotten yourself in the right frame of mind?
2. Have you trained your voice—not strained it?
3. Are you paying attention to your appearance?
4. Have you practiced what you want to say?
5. Are you ready to own your audience?

Now that you're all geared up to step out into the spotlight, it's time to see what happens should the proverbial tomatoes start lobbing at you. Turn to *preempt* to learn how to "duck" and dodge any and all distractions and distracters.

The Bottom Line

Acting or singing, presenting or having a one-on-one with someone at your office—it's all about performance. A good performance wins raves with critic and fans, a poor one can jettison a performer into obscurity. The same goes for the business world. Just a lackluster conference or meeting, or even conversation in the corridor, can knock you off the path to success. But a stellar one can shoot you right up through the ranks. For that reason, always conduct yourself as if the curtain has gone up and it's your time to shine.

STRATEGY 5

PREEMPT: Squashing Out the "No"

**"You cannot simultaneously prevent
and prepare for war."
—Albert Einstein**

Einstein was a genius, there's no denying it. But even geniuses can be wrong sometimes, and when it comes to the guerilla warfare known as 21st century communications, he's actually a bit off-base with this remark. To be fair, Einstein never had to compete with cell phones and BlackBerrys and 21st century attention spans when he addressed people. So how could he know, as we are learning in this crazy age, that the only way to prevent battle is to prepare?

Surely you've been there—we've all been there. You enter a room, ready to speak, thinking you're fully prepared for the worst to happen. And then something crops up that you never expected, and your whole presentation goes to hell. Maybe the speech you planned was for another age group—and you were given the wrong information about your audience from the conference planner. Maybe the day you've finally gotten it together to confront your boss for a raise, her dog dies and she's in pieces.

In the real world, many things are not in your control. You may not always know the order in which you are to present at a conference until the last minute. You have to get approval for your presentation and your slides. In fact, in some industries all material must go through regulatory, legal, public affairs before you're able to stand and deliver. The day comes and you may still be waiting final approval. It's enough to make you want to throw up your hands and call it quits.

Throughout this book, I've included Rabbit Tricks and plans of attack to handle these hiccups as they've cropped up. Think of this chapter as a giant bag of tricks and attack strategies to help you every step of the way.

Even when you think you're prepared, you always need to think past "What's the worst that can happen?" We tend to wing it a lot these days. We're busy, so we spend less time planning and more time firefighting. It's as if we feel that, as long as we have a checklist of the bare essentials, we can handle whatever comes.

It's not enough.

There are so many wild events that can spark from just one event. Think of it as chaos theory, or the domino effect. I've spent years in the control room of TV stations where there's more than a little stress. You have time to fill, dead air to avoid, commercials to air, a director barking orders into the ear piece of the interviewer, teleprompters, camera persons—a virtual Petrie dish of potential mishaps. If you've ever noticed a gaffe made by an on-air reporter, I'll bet you that you then saw two more mishaps happen in quick succession. A newsperson coughs on air, then mispronounces a word, then as the anxiety builds in the studio, the segment ends prematurely as the station goes to commercial.

And that's an event to which we can all relate. Think of the last time you were at a meeting and preparing to show your slides. The power cord for your laptop wouldn't reach the wall socket, so you had to run your computer off the battery. You're nervous, and you open up the wrong document. So now a memo you were writing about work conditions is being beamed up on the wall. Been there, done that.

And because you think nothing else will go right, your own sense of doubt begins to disengage you. In today's world, an unexpected crisis only leads to more chaos. One thing going wrong—and sparking a string of disasters—is worse now than ever before because there is no cushion of time built in to get things under control and then reverse a series of unfortunate events as they occur.

Every day in business, you're in the throes of a potential crisis. We have too much information, but not enough knowledge. Unfortunately, people focus on the task at hand when the task is in their hands, and not hours and days before. If you want to survive out there, that's not going to be enough. You need to think outside what you've been asked to do. You need to stop expecting information will come to you, and go out and get it.

A large part of work life involves teamwork and decision-making by consensus. In the process, we encounter a wide range of personalities, personal agendas, and idiosyncratic behaviors, some of them likable, some merely tolerable, and some of the sort that, if we had the choice, we would gladly avoid. These last difficult people seem to take a particular pleasure in embarrassing their colleagues, and generally disrupting communications with their own brand of noise. All too often, all it takes is for one "heckler" or passive-aggressive critic to infect others with skepticism and doubt, and shoot your credibility in the foot. Even in a one-on-one scenario, a speaker can loose his or her listener when an unexpected pushback comes that wasn't anticipated. But you can minimize—even eliminate—their negative effects in meetings if you maintain your composure, and manage around them or through them.

NOISE BLASTER!

Always remember two words: focus and control. Everyone wants to be in control of the discussion, but only one person can be—and that person should be you. Focus on your key points. Focus on the audience's needs. Focus on the agenda, and bring the topic back to your agenda when it goes off point (more on that later).

This chapter will give you the tools you need to keep your composure—even in the most disastrous situations—and keep your listeners under control. In this chapter, you will:

- ¤ learn to anticipate disaster before it strikes.
- ¤ isolate interruptions before they send you spiraling out of control.

¤   "bridge" your answers back to your agenda when someone tries to throw you off track.

¤   make a graceful exit, even in the most disastrous situations.

TIPS FROM THE TRENCHES

Patricia Diaz Dennis

chair of the National Board of Directors for Girl Scouts of the USA, senior vice president and assistant general counsel for AT&T Inc.

"I remember the days when people spent their leisure time reading books, going to the theater, or visiting a museum. Their activities were reflected in the vibrancy of our language. Nowadays, people don't seem to be as interested in these kinds of things, opting instead for video games and other modes of electronic entertainment.

"The result is a lack of a vocabulary to use when communicating. I find many young people do not express themselves well. E-mail, IM, and text messages are ubiquitous, replacing face-to-face communication. Don't get me wrong, I love how fast and easy electronic communication is, but many people don't stop and think about what they are typing, from either emotional or grammatical standpoints. It shocks me when I read what some young lawyers write today, and these are educated people!

"In addition, the fractionalization of the media is causing less common ground for all of us. There is so much variety now, and every niche audience has something in which to indulge its interest, which is great! Diversity is flourishing. However, the flip side is that we aren't all connected by watching the same newscasts or reading the same newspapers anymore. There's less in this new world that unites us and more that divides us.

"Getting a point across to a diverse audience is more difficult now than ever before because we don't share universal experiences on which we can draw. I find this lack of shared experience true as a speaker and from attending speaking events. So, I work very hard to be informed about all kinds of issues outside of my own personal and professional sphere of influence. We all must make a concerted effort to become engaged in the world of our neighbors. We must think expansively. Without a developed vocabulary and an interest in the rest of the world, we cannot link up with our audience. These skills are what we teach the girls involved in Girl Scouting because they are important for effective communication, and also for responsible citizenship if we ever hope to solve the social and economic problems of this world.

Be Prepared for *Anything*

No matter the size of your audience, you need to anticipate fallout from the discussion before you begin. Say you're having a meeting with your boss. It's possible your boss will be called out of the room on an urgent matter—more urgent than yours. If you're conducting a meeting, someone could have a chip on his shoulder and believe his only purpose in life, at least for that hour, is to negate every point you make. In a large group, someone's cell phone could keep going off—or maybe a fire drill gets called right in the middle of your bottom line.

For a normal presentation, you should expect that things will go wrong, and take action before that point in order to prevent certain events from occurring. Following is a checklist of elements to have in place before you arrive.

Preemptive Presentation To-Do List

- ⌑ Wherever you're going, tell that person who booked you that you plan to arrive an hour earlier than planned.

- ⌑ Make sure you have access to a printer and set up your own equipment if possible.

- ⌑ Make sure your hotel has a 24-hour ability to print documents for you.

- ⌑ Even if you're in your own city, find out who in the neighborhood can print for you should your own equipment fail you.

- ⌑ Write down all pertinent information about the place to which you're going to connect—address, directions, phone number of contact person—on the front of the file folder.

- ⌑ Think about what could possibly go wrong (from an audience member getting sick to the Apocalypse) and think of how you can thwart any distraction that gets in the way of your message being delivered to your audience.

Scaling New Horizons

In this day and age of global travel, jetlag is one of the main factors that's going to trip you up when you present. How can you manage?

- ⋈ Avoid alcohol.
- ⋈ Drink plenty of water.
- ⋈ While you're flying, walk around and get exercise, and bend from the waist.
- ⋈ Take long, deep breaths.

Additionally, be prepared for your checked luggage to get lost in transit. Include in your carryon suitcase a toiletries bag with security regulation-size toothpaste, makeup or shaving depilatory, contact lens solution, and critical medication. Take also a set of underwear and fresh shirt and dress shoes. If your luggage doesn't make it to your destination the same time you do, you may not look elegant for your presentation, but at least you'll be well groomed.

NOISE BLASTER!

Always take a second's pause before answering *any* question. That way, when a question does stump you, and you need to take time to answer, it won't look obvious that you don't know.

A Crisis for the Coach

My professional life is an endless string of last-minute phone calls and drop-and-run, on-the-moment traveling. It would be wonderful for me to get the information I need to develop audience-motivating messages several weeks in advance, so I can take the time to process it using all my strategies, but that's not always realistic in today's high-speed business environment.

Sometimes I get less than 24 hours notice. I fly into a new city at midnight, where the material I need to prepare for an early morning meeting is waiting for me in my e-mail inbox. You probably know it's not easy to find an open business center in a hotel that late at night. I can't tell you how many times I've brought a memory stick down to the front desk, begging and pleading with the clerk to print out my documents for me.

I remember one assignment that had all the ingredients for a disaster due to freakish weather. If it was January or February or even March, you'd probably factor in snow and ice to your planning. But at the end of April? Yet, it happened during one of my assignments. A raging blizzard. In April.

I was there to do coaching in the afternoon, but by mid-morning my audience was becoming ever more nervous about flying home from the convention site. I had prepared a series of presentation skills workshops for 200 employees from around the world who worked for financial services firm. There were going to be 10 concurrent workshops, with one member of my team leading each breakout group. The session was to take place after lunch.

As we were walking to the breakout rooms, a staffer from the client organization approached me and said that people were panicking and trying to reschedule their flights. They were down to 100 people, shortening the sessions from three hours to two, and now using five rooms instead of 10.

I set about reorganizing my team and our agenda. I took 10 steps forward, and was continuing on my way to the rooms when a staffer from another agency involved with the conference ran up to me and said, "We have to shrink the sessions by one more room." I readjusted the team again and kept walking.

Not two minutes later a man I'd never met or seen before jumped out at me and barked, "You're doing the program in the main room to the whole group and you have 10 minutes to get it together. Oh, and you're presentation slot is now 15 minutes—not a minute longer."

I took a deep breath and a step backward and surveyed this bundle of nerves. This director, who I'm sure must be delightful at a party, was riddled with anxiety, because he was losing control of the meeting he had spent six months planning, and now he was taking it out on his staff…and on mine.

By this point, I basically had about five minutes to reorganize my information. We needed to design slides and choose a presenter who would be able to inspire and train an audience in presentation skills—and do this in 1/10 of the allocated time. Plus, I was dealing with a maniac who was in a complete panic over having his neck on the line. So every minute of that five minutes, he'd come in, bark something incoherent, and run out again.

There was no time to think—no time to plan. This was the time to go with gut instincts.

I borrowed a laptop from the production crew, chose a creative and quick thinker from my team, and suggested to him what slides would be best. While that was going on I thought for a moment about the audience now, a hostile one because these were the folks who couldn't get their flights changed and were stuck in the city overnight. Not the best crowd you'd ever want to perform in front of. I selected a colleague who is large in stature, has a big voice, and a powerful command of people and subject matter.

We reviewed our bottom-line messages two or three times and then rehearsed in the few minutes remaining. He then walked on stage, took a breath, and opened the presentation with a relevant anecdote from the morning's general session. I hovered in the front row giving him hand signals to keep him to the tight time schedule.

Did we pull it off? Hugely. But it worked only because we allowed our experience and knowledge of audience behavior to guide us.

NOISE BLASTER!

Eye contact is your best weapon in Q&A warfare. You can cue a person to speak and dismiss them just by using your eyes contact.

TOUGH-LOVE TURNAROUND: REALITY CHECK

You say: But I'm the boss; I should know all the facts about everything here.

I say: What?!. Your people already know you don't know everything. You're not expected to know everything. What you are expected to do is listen and guide the people who do know everything.

There's nothing more annoying to people who know things than for you to pretend you know the things they know—when you don't. You'll get in good with your people when you tell them you rely on their knowledge of certain subjects, and that you expect them to speak up about issues, challenges, and opportunities. And stop micromanaging. In fact, you may even consider giving them a speak-back mechanism for making them feel comfortable when they tell you things you should know. Consider an anonymous forum, which can provide your people the opportunity to speak their minds without fear of recrimination should their views go against yours.

TIPS FROM THE TRENCHES

Cherie Marshall, PsyD
psychologist and life coach

"Through the years I have learned a trick to handle the 'discounters,' those people who are out to discount your point as a speaker, often the main point of the talk!

"A simple formula can get you back on track with minimal effort, and elevate your main point back to level ground: Acknowledge what the speaker has said: 'What you're saying about such and such is a good point.' Then segue back to your point. All it takes is one magic word: nonetheless. Then you can Bridge right back to your point. It works every time."

Minimizing Disruptions

These days, heckling has become more common than ever. My theory is that it's because we live in a YouTube culture. The prevailing mentality is that everything is up for discussion and voting is welcome. For that reason, it has actually become trendy to be more challenging in meetings, at community events, and in entertainment venues.

So, expect to be challenged. In fact, you may start to look forward to it. There's nothing quite as exhilarating in a meeting as a person who tries to derail you while you remain calm, and carefully, methodically, and collegiately dispute their statements.

For that reason, it's hugely important that you back up everything you say with heavy substance. If you're not knowledgeable, they will find your vulnerabilities and exploit the situation. If your data's full of holes, that person will find those holes and keep digging. Wrap yourself in your facts. Wear your facts. If you're knowledgeable, they'll eventually get bored and stop picking; if you're not, you'll end up with zero "stars," zero credibility, and zero impact.

Staying Grounded

When the undeserved allegations come flying at you out of nowhere, stay focused and stay in the present. Avoid thinking about the knot in your stomach or your escalating heartbeat. Listen to the person with a calm expression on your face. Do not tense up. Keep breathing and then say, "Chris, the data you reference actually refers to data I'm going to discuss in a minute." As you are saying this, redirect your eyes and the angle of your body away from the questioner and onto the rest of the audience. By your nonverbal behavior, you're cueing the questioner out.

When you silence your saboteur, just be sure you make them feel valued. "Roger, while I appreciate your interest in that, it's unfortunate that we don't really have time to talk about it today. Let's talk offline later as we have a jam-packed agenda to get through."

You can also pull someone else in when a question goes out of your comfort zone of what you know, and enlist an ally to redirect it. "That's a great point, Maria, but I think Sam may be better equipped to get that answer for you. I'll introduce you two at the end of my presentation."

Sometimes people don't mean any harm when they throw off your presentation. They just feel the need to contribute. They're not really listening to you and want to speak, so they'll ask you myriad irrelevant questions. Harmless as they can be, however, they will throw you off your game, distract your audience, and they need to be stopped. After the first couple of questions, your audience will likely get annoyed and look to you to bail them out. Take action.

Whatever you do, don't lose your cool. Ever. Never let it get to a point that you're visibly angry. If you're a very expressive person, it will show, so do whatever you can to hide it. You don't ever want to lose control. If you do lose control, you're not likely to ever get it back. Once you've lost control of the room, your presentation is doomed. Not only will you have wasted your time by spending an hour or so not getting your point across, you'll lose credibility when you get lose your temper. That's the main reason why preempting is so important.

Stay the Course

There are seven places you can communicate your key messages during your presentation:

1. Grabber.
2. Bottom-line.
3. Facts.
4. Anecdotal support.
5. Visuals.
6. Q&A
7. Summary.

Getting a Grip (on Your Audience)

Most simple, direct questions are best handled with a simple, direct answer, even if that answer happens to be: "I don't know, but I'll find the information and get back to you," or "I'll put you in touch with someone who knows the answer."

Other questions are designed to lead the unsuspecting answerer down paths best avoided. Your best protection in those situations is to recognize them for what they are and know how to take control.

Controlling Q&A is easier than you might think once you analyze the form that questions often take.

The Limited-Options Query

This is when the questioner gives you only two choices for an answer. "Are you going shopping today or staying home to read?" "Are you more interested in profits or clean air?" In a casual, relaxed conversation, we don't feel threatened or defensive and will either pick one of the choices or volunteer a third choice. But in a stressful, more formal environment, we may feel put on the spot and find ourselves getting forced into an answer we'd otherwise not choose. Stay your ground. Take a pause before answering and then say, "Actually, I'm…" and go for the answer that you believe in.

The What-If Query

For some reason, when we are asked to speculate a future outcome, we often jump into that fire pit. There's no surer way to lose control of Q&A than to start answering hypothetical questions. "So, if you're elected President, the country will be 100-percent safe and prosperous?" "What if this new-fangled diet doesn't work and we gain all our weight back?" You'll never be comfortable if you make future guarantees. Always, always answer this type of questioning technique with data from the present or from the past. We can only guarantee solutions that we know unequivocally are true. If you start, answering one hypothetical question you will find yourself besieged with numerous follow-up questions, with each one putting you deeper and deeper in a hole.

The Run-On Query

This is the kind of question that has no real beginning, middle, or end. It's illogical. It's usually asked by someone who hasn't taken a minute to get her thoughts together and speaks parenthetically. "The other day when I was walking by the school playground I saw the big hole that Jane fell into a few years ago. I saw her the other day. Her daughter is going out with my son. He's an orthodontist..." Get the point?

It's a touchy situation because you don't want to be rude and say, "Huh? Do you have a question within that statement?" But the longer the person talks, the more off-putting it becomes. The time is ticking away, everyone else has questions, and now the tension is filling the air. What do you do?

Wait 30 seconds. If you don't hear a question somewhere in that rambling statement, take the reins in your hand by using the person's name (everyone stops for a split second when they hear their name). Then, using some of the words that the rambler is using, think about what the question might be and offer an answer or opinion: "That's very interesting. Let's get together later and chat more about that." Then move your eyes to another potential questioner and say, "Joe, I believe I saw your hand up what is your question."

Managing Conflict

¤   Diffuse opposition by narrowing the areas of apparent conflict.

¤   Get adversaries to agree that the objective is similar, even if the solutions differ.

¤   Provide room for choice, so that adversaries can feel they have participated in the final outcome.

¤   Acknowledge your opponents' feelings, and agree that they should be dealt with.

¤   Demonstrate respect for and understanding of the other side's position.

¤   Restate the opponent's objection to see if he remains firm or is willing to back off.

¤   Leave on a high note.

Bridging is the best technique for bringing your audience back to focus, and back on your topic. We'll get more into this essential technique in a little bit.

"You have to learn how to duck, because they're gonna throw it at you."
—Arthur Miller, writer

Dealing With Difficult People

Even with the best intentions, your presentation will be filled with rhetorical landmines—people throwing your point off track with their own misdirected contributions—and internal combustion—the frustration about being at this meeting seething beneath the surface, that may have nothing at all to do with you. Following are the kinds of people you need to look out for and ways to diffuse them.

The Gotcha Guy

This is the person who thrives on making you feel powerless and vulnerable.

You have the key slot at The Big Meeting. Your colleague, who was passed over for that slot, is now offended and ready to make you pay. Just as you're about to start your well-rehearsed presentation, the Gotcha Guy yells from the back of the room: "Hey, Joe, are you going to fall apart like the last time?"

You go pale. Your knees buckle. You start to perspire. You want to run away. Don't. There is a population out there that thrives on the vulnerability of others and keeping them off balance. They like to watch you squirm, to see you fold under pressure. They get off on mind games.

So what do you do? For one, don't respond. You may find yourself smiling self-consciously, or involuntarily offering a return quip. Don't. Find your equilibrium. Keep your dignity. You take away their power if you don't respond.

Instead, take a deep breath. Pause. Wait two seconds and look forward. Speak your introduction. Stay in the present. Don't think about Gotcha Guy, think only about the prize: doing well. You'll be a star.

The Manipulator

This is the person who gains power by moving the players (meaning you) around the chess board. He gains power by manipulating others.

You are a district manager on the sales force. The regional manager (RM) is attempting to stimulate revenues and, in so doing, increase his own bonus. It's a competitive environment; everyone's fighting for the same bonus dollars.

In a meeting with 100 colleagues, the RM says to you: "Joe, why don't you tell Mike how you increased your district's revenues. What's your strategy? I'm sure he'll benefit from your tips."

You feel set up. This is not the time to offer out your strategy, as helpful as your strategy might be. You need time to think it through.

Take a deep breath before you respond, and say: "I will have to give it some thought. Mike, why don't you and I meet offline to talk about it." In that way, you'll deflect the tension in the room, you'll put the onus on Mike, and you won't have to spill out unorganized thoughts.

The Big Dog in the Room

This is the person who constantly has to "mark" her or his spot in the meeting.

You're meeting with your team to update your activities. You've worked long and hard getting your facts just right. Your slides are ready, you've rehearsed, and you feel competent. The team is seated around a conference table. You are at your laptop and projecting your slides on the screen. Big Dog stands up, walks over to you, and proceeds to hover right over you as you speak. And then, every time you open your mouth, he interrupts: "Hey, Joe, you need to know…" and, "Hey, you haven't included…" and, "Look, you missed an important…" or, "Twenty years ago, when I was…" The drama is intense. Everyone is agitated, including you.

Don't panic. Be confident that you have done your job well and sit quietly. Let the person run out of steam and then calmly and cooly say: "Thank you for your input. As you can see, my research shows…" or, "In my experience…" or, "Actually, the report suggests…" and follow it up with details of your findings in a clear, direct, succinct manner. Then return to the remainder of your presentation.

The Mumster

This is the person who has information you need, but decides not to share it with the rest of the group. It could be a power play, or it could be that he or she feels self-conscious or inadequate.

There are two ways to handle the Mumster. If he or she usually withholds information as a power play, your best bet is to meet with him or her alone prior to the meeting. Building a relationship before the meeting will result in the most successful outcome.

If you know the Mumster doesn't usually speak because he or she is shy, connect with him or her several days in advance and let the person know you'll be calling on them. During the meeting, you can try doing a "go around," where you ask everyone for input and the final person you ask is the person in question. This will allow the Mumster to collect his or her thoughts and build his or her confidence.

The Grenade

This is the person who shuts down a meeting with a caustic comment, or tries to move it to her agenda. This person will try to monopolize your event.

The Grenade waits until the meeting is on a roll. New ideas are being formulated, discussions are robust, but the meeting is not going the way the Grenade wants it to go, and so she needs to push it in his direction. With one explosive comment from the Grenade, your work could be in jeopardy.

If you feel you can adequately handle the argument at the time the Grenade makes it, you could speak to it at the moment. Or you could say, "I know you feel strongly about this, however, we have all agreed to stay on point. Why don't you and I discuss your issues after the meeting?"

The Yes'um

This is the person who nods affirmatively the whole time you're talking. He volunteers to take on tasks to look good in front of everyone in the room, but never follows through. At the 11th hour, when you're stuck, this is the person who will wiggle out of helping you by saying: "That's not what I understood," or "Remember I spoke to you in the hall about it?"

To deal with these people, always get their commitment through e-mail and establish a due date they agree to in writing. You might also list their name along with everyone else's on a white board, with due dates in the next column, and a third column for checkmarks indicating the deadline has been met. When everyone else's due date has arrived, and checkmarks made, the yes'um will probably feel pressure to abide to the commitment made, and will likely think twice before mindlessly nodding at your next meeting.

In any of the situations mentioned, move your eyes away from the person who's annoying you and break the magnetic pull. Swivel your body away in another direction and focus on someone else. Look for something wider than right in front of you.

NOISE BLASTER!

Most people feel they work too hard and are undervalued. When you can, take your people aside individually, pat them on the back, and say: "Hey, I think you're doing a really good job."

RABBIT TRICK
WAKING THE DEAD

Problem: The person or people to whom you're talking look as though they're about to pass out from boredom or exhaustion or whatever—it doesn't really matter why, the only thing that matters is that you resuscitate your audience. And quickly!

Solution: Engage! Engage! Engage! The is the best CPR for an audience of zombies. It's also a great opportunity for a little post-preparation probing. If you're speaking to a group, start asking questions that involve an active response. "Please, a show of hands, how many of you saw *Dancing With the Stars Last Night*?" or, "How many of you remember the TV show *M*A*S*H*?" or, "Who likes to watch *The Office*?" Ideally, you want to tailor your questions to the topic at hand, but as that could be anything, I'm making it as general as possible here. For a larger, sleepy group, take it a step (or stand) further: "If you're originally from this city, please stand" or, "If you support breast cancer research, please stand with me and take a moment, to take a stand against the disease and also show our support for the people we know who have been affected." Okay, a bit dramatic, but who's going to be able to snooze through that?

The trickiest situation is when there are only one or two people pretending to be listening to you as they nod sleepily after everything you say. In this case, you must act immediately. Engage them on a personal level, and without being intrusive. Switch the topic to ask questions about their lives, and try and relate things directly to them. "Janet, how's your home renovation going? You know, this company has an interiors division. Maybe someone there can give you some advice." You may even suggest taking a coffee break from the meeting—and offering to buy the coffee.

"Some people have such a talent for making the best of a bad situation that they go around creating bad situations so they can make the best of them."
——Jean Kerr, writer

Cross That Bridge

"Bridging" is an essential skill for anyone who needs to relay information without letting others throw them off track. It's the best way to deflect a negative question and use its energy to redirect the discussion toward answers that project positive solutions and conclusions.

Bridging is actually a technique we use every day, though most of the time, we aren't even aware that we're doing it. In casual conversation, we swipe the spotlight from each other all the time: "That movie reminds me of a book I'm reading." So the conversation was about a movie and now it's flipped to a book. It's so simplistic and so ordinary, so unconscious in natural conversation.

TIPS FROM THE TRENCHES

Donna Ramer
president of Strategcations

"Risk-taking and knowledge are the keys to pulling rabbits out of hats. For example, as volunteer chair of communications for one of the country's largest nonprofit organizations, I was scheduled to present a resolution for funds to research corporate support from a specific type of company. But when I walked to the podium and the secretary read the resolution, I found it had been inappropriately altered by one person who disagreed with our research.

Although I was seething inside, I quickly decided to take a risk: I turned to the association's president and then back to the eight-plus members of the board and asked them to vote against the resolution and consider the original, which I reconstructed from my notes.

It worked, mostly because I kept my cool, understood what I was talking about, and decided to take a risk. Two years later, the associate was the recipient of a grant for tens of thousands of dollars for a public education campaign.

But it's in situations in which the conversation doesn't flow so naturally, when stress is high and comfort is low, when it's most needed. If you need to defend what you're saying, perhaps if you're being upstaged, your reaction to the challenge may make you defensive. And that's not what you want at all, as being defensive makes you look guilty—guilty of something of which you're being accused, or of not knowing something you're supposed to know. It's very natural to go on the defensive when we're challenged, but if you're looking to make a point with someone, you're only going to trip yourself up if you get defensive.

Bridging neutralizes controversy. It doesn't agree with any statements; it doesn't put anyone on the defensive. It simply moves the subject to a key message of yours.

Say you're talking about a new benefits initiative and someone in the audience snidely remarks that the last plan you proposed was ridiculously inadequate—and why should we listen to you about this plan? Of course your first—and very human—inclination is to snap back, "How dare you say or ask such a thing to me?" Or, at the very least, you retreat from your position of strength, protecting yourself as you exclaim: "No, that's not true!"

But if you do that, if you react without thinking, you'll lose a golden opportunity not only to regain your focus and footing, but to enforce your point: "Actually, this new plan, just launched this summer, is superior to the last because…" or, "The gold standard with benefit packages actually does support my conclusion because..." and, "Actually, the new equipment does fit into the budget, and here's why…" and so forth.

Instead of tripping you up, a wayward question can sometimes actually be answered to help cement your point.

In Bridging, when someone asks you a question, it's not the direct answer to that question that you necessarily need to focus on; it's where that person's question can take you. Is the question veering off the agenda? Will it interrupt the flow of information you've worked so hard to construct? Will it open a can of worms you're not equipped to reseal? If the answer to any of these is yes, than it's time to Bridge—and Bridge fast!

To Bridge successfully, you have to appear to answer the question, even if the answer is not directly related to the question that was asked, but you also have to bring it to the next level. A speaker has roughly 30 seconds to answer a negative, cross the Bridge, and retake the high ground before the audience's impatience typically kicks in, so there's no time here for uncertainty or waffling.

Also, in today's highly impatient, sophisticated, and jaded environment, people see right through dishonesty. So you also have to keep it on the level.

Bridge-Building Tool Kit

Keep these bridging phrases in your memory and pull them out when you face a high-stress situation:

- "What's unique here..."
- "Another addition to..."
- "What I have found in my experience..."
- "The data clearly show..."
- "It's important/vital/critical to point out..."

A few years ago, I watched a pilot on a talk show try to encourage young people to go into the aviation field. He was an excellent at Bridging. He didn't just pull answers out of can, such as "You get to see the world"; he used solid examples. "Last year, I was assigned for six weeks in the Caribbean." The pilot made the situation more interesting by allowing his listener to visualize him there—and themselves as well. That kind of relate-ability helps keep listeners engaged.

It's essential in Bridging that you allow your own personality to come through. It not only builds credibility, it draws people to you. Bridging keeps meetings on track and validates the opinions, attitudes, and productivity of meetings. The technique helps keep everything safe. Especially when it comes to dealing with reporters.

NOISE BLASTER!

Never think of the process of giving an interview as "I am being interviewed." That's passive. You need to reverse it. Remember, it's not what they ask, but how you answer that will ultimately drive the story.

Paul's Prickly PR Pickle

Paul had just landed his dream job. He was now head of the PR division of the aeronautics company he had joined right out of school, and had worked his way to the top from marketing assistant in fewer than eight years. Everything was golden.

And then the bottom fell out.

There were allegations about shoddy workmanship on a new airplane model. The new super high-speed, fuel-efficient model was being criticized by industry pundits for being thrown together and put in the sky before all the kinks had been worked out.

There hadn't been a crash yet, but during a TV interview, Paul found himself experiencing an interview crash.

In the middle of the interview, the reporter asked Paul about the workmanship. Paul prepared for this answer by giving supporting data about extensive testing.

The reporter went on and asked other questions, and suddenly circled back to the workmanship issue. Paul answered the question again. And then suddenly the camera "broke down." (This is actually a true manipulative trick used by reporters to trip their subjects. I used to be in journalism. Enough said.)

While the camera was being replaced, the reporter again asked the question and Paul answered exactly the same way again. The reporter asked again, and again Paul answered in the same way.

As I told Paul during our coaching session, reporters will come back to the same question two or three ways, and will ask it two or three times—until they're convinced they got as much answer as you're going to let go.

The PS on this story is that after the interview, as the reporter walked Paul to the elevator, he asked the question again. Paul answered just the same way. The reporter then shook Paul's hand and said, "Wow, you're good."

The spot aired. Paul's short, concise answer was included. Of course, the opposing viewpoint was also included. But the key here is that Paul got his message through clearly, succinctly, and effectively.

NOISE BLASTER!

If a reporter or any other questioner tries to incite you: "Surely you don't mean that! How can you say this?" you have to stay true to your answer; you can't start changing the script. If they smell fear or lack of confidence, they'll keep digging, so stick to your guns and keep answering their same questions over and over again the same way.

Slanting It in *Your* Direction

Your boss has just named you the new public spokesperson for a new initiative in your company. Or perhaps, less formally, the local *Gazette* wants to talk to you about something in which your company is involved—a specific project you're working on. In this instance, talking to the media is a necessary evil, but that doesn't mean you need to pull to the dark side. The trick is for you to be the one controlling the interview, not the reporter. Here are some tricks to use to keep the article focused on your agenda:

⌘ **Consult the pros.** If your organization has a public relations department, check in with them on advice for dealing with the media.

⌘ **Know your business.** You want to have a firm understanding of the product or policy before discussing it outside the company.

⌘ **Know your interviewer.** Having a keen understanding of the publication that will be calling upon you will help you better know how to answer questions the way his readers might like them answered.

⌘ **Always call back.** Never let an interviewer ambush you by talking you into giving an interview on their terms. When they call, put them off. "Yes, I am the spokesperson. I would be happy to talk to you. I'm in a meeting—let me call you back." This is your first control. This is how you take the reins. And when you do return the call, call back the general number and find out if that person actually even works for that publication.

⊠ **Validate.** Before you call the reporter back, go back and check your facts. Be sure you have all the facts correct and that all the points you want to make have been (and remain) approved.

⊠ **Rehearse.** You should not be reading from a script, but if you must, rehearse it many times so you won't come off sounding like you are.

⊠ **Imagine.** Think up some questions the reporter will probably be asking you and practice answering them out loud.

⊠ **Stop and breathe.** Don't run through your practice answers like a speeding train. Take breaths. Pause from time to time as if you're thinking of the words as you're saying them.

⊠ **In your words.** Sometimes the words a company will give its spokesperson to say are not words that person would use, and if they're spoken verbatim, they sound like words put in the mouth. If this happens to you, try to change the words to ones you would use, but be absolutely careful about preserving the meaning.

⊠ **Cut it down.** If any sentences are more than eight to 10 words, chop them down. In oral communication, it's natural to use fewer words than more because, pauses aside, we can't see punctuation to take a break from listening.

⊠ **No mystery words.** Will they know what you're talking about? Whatever messages you've decided on, make sure they're easily understood using laymen's terms. Just because he's interviewing you doesn't mean he's taken the time to get to know you and your product. If you leave the translation up to him, you might not get the most accurate outcome.

⋈ **Listen up.** Be sure you get the full question before you answer. If you don't hear the question, be sure the reporter repeats it for you. Your reason for being interviewed is to provide your company's perspective and some quotable phrase. And remember: Nothing is ever "off the record."

⋈ **Loud and clear.** Try not to use the speaker phone if you can help it. Stand up and gesture as if you're doing a presentation, and speak slowly and clearly. Reply in clear, crisp, linear words and sentences—leaving nothing to chance. You can bet the person on the other end of the phone will be typing while you talk, so give him or her a chance to get all the right information down.

⋈ **Bridge.** When a reporter hits a hot button, load your first answer with the heartbeat message. When he asks: "What's this going to cost?" Tell him: "I certainly want to answer your question, but let me first give you some perspective and bring you up to date." Go into your core message then and give a snapshot of the big picture as you want it to be seen.

⋈ **See the end.** A reporter will try to keep you on the phone as long as possible, but when you feel you've exhausted the subject matter, the interview should be over.

⋈ **Instant replay.** Reporters will often repeat back to you what they're insisting. "So what you're saying is...." If the reporter is changing the meaning of your statement, clarify and correct. Most reporters really do want to get it right.

⌷ **And repeat!** When you come to the end of an interview, take the opportunity to reinforce your main idea. When a reporter asks, "Do you have anything to add?" your answer should always be yes. Repeat something important. "The main issue is," "The most important aspect is," "The reason consumers will rally around this is," and so forth. Even if the reporter doesn't ask, add: "Just to make sure I've made myself clear," then launch into the important message.

What *Never* to Say to a Reporter

It's a reporter's job to get as much information from you as possible, and this means he or she can and will ask you just about anything imaginable. So, avoid using these phrases at all costs when being interviewed:

⌷ "I shouldn't be saying this, but..."
⌷ "My competition may tell you otherwise, but..."
⌷ "I know the authorities have suspected..."
⌷ "Everything I've just told you has been off the record..."
⌷ "That's not the not right question, here's the right question..."

NOISE BLASTER!

It's rare you'll ever get a reporter's questions in advance. But what you can ask for and should get is general area of questioning.

The Bottom Line

Even when all your best plans start falling apart in front of you, you can still make the best of a bad situation and even come out on top. What it all comes down to is that more sweat equals less blood. More preparation means the likelihood of getting thrown to the wolves will greatly diminish. Smart communicators have an arsenal of contingency plans to help them respond calmly and confidently to any communications crisis. Follow the lessons of this chapter, and you can count yourself among them.

New Millennium virtual board meeting.

Preempt: At a Glance

1. Did you consider all the variables that might come into play when you deliver a message to anyone?
2. Have you prepared contingency plans B, C, and D?
3. Are you ready to deal with hecklers and others who will try to pull attention away from you and twist your agenda?
4. Will you handle these people without losing your composure?
5. Can you walk away with your dignity when the situation becomes utterly unsalvageable?

Now that you've learned to analyze your audience, organize your information in the most palatable way possible, present yourself as a person to whom they need to listen, and deliver that message in an effective way, taking into account any an all obstacles you may encounter; you're ready to face the world and finally start getting what you want from others. Good luck!

INDEX

ABOUT THE AUTHOR

Karen Berg, CEO of CommCore Strategies, is a communication strategist, international speaker, and executive coach who has prepared thousands of professionals for crisis management, shareholders meetings, management presentations, government and expert witness testimony, product launch campaigns, media interviews, and more. Coauthor of the best-seller *Get to the Point* (Kendal Hunt, 1995), Berg is a recognized industry trendsetter whose views on communications issues have been featured in *The New York Times*, *The Wall Street Journal*, *Forbes*, *Redbook*, *Working Woman*, *McCall's,* and other publications. Frequently interviewed on communication trends, she has appeared on CNN, CNBC, and Today in New York. Berg makes her home in New York when she is not traveling on assignment.